POWER-GLIDE
FOREIGN
LANGUAGE COURSES

Power-Glide
Children's French Level III

Activity Book

by

Robert W. Blair

This product would not have been possible without the assistance of many people. The help of those mentioned below was invaluable.

Editorial, Design and Production Staff
Instructional Design: Robert Blair, Ph.D.
Project Coordinator: James Blair
Development Manager: David Higginbotham
Story Writer: Natalie Prado
Cover Design: Guy Francis
Contributing Editors: Gretchen Hilton, Emily Spackman, Ann Dee Knight, Heather Monson, Amelia Taylor
Audio Voices: Ali Seable Durham, Erin Sorensen, Peter Enyeart, Art Burnah, Christel Marie Secrist, David Higginbotham
Illustrator: Apryl Robertson
Translators: Christel Marie Secrist
Musicians: Geoff Groberg, Rob Bird
Audio Recording, Editing and Mixing: Rob Bird

© 2002 Power-Glide. All rights reserved.
Printed in the United States of America
ISBN 1-58204-101-6

No part of this publication may be reproduced, stored in a retrieval system, or transmitted, in any form or by any means, electronic, mechanical, recording, or otherwise without the prior written permission of Power-Glide.

Power-Glide Foreign Language Courses
1682 W 820 N, Provo, UT 84601
(2/02)

Contents

Introduction	4
The Adventure Continues	8
Diglot Weave Review	10
Promenons-nous dans les bois	12
J'ai perdu le do ma clarinette	15
The Three Bears I	
Scatter Chart	18
Diglot Weave	20
Review Questions	25
The Three Bears II	
Diglot Weave	26
Story Telling	29
Word Puzzle 1	32
The Dog, the Cat and the Mouse I	
Scatter Chart	34
Diglot Weave	35
The Dog, the Cat and the Mouse II	
Diglot Weave	37
Story Telling	41
Word Puzzle 2	43
Hard Days	
Horseshoe Story	44
Scatter Chart	45
Story Telling	46
Mystery Map	48
Paintings!	50
Test 1	52
Answer Key	56
The Adventure Continues	58
Fais dodo, Colas, mon petit frére	59
Lundi Matin	61
The Hunter and the Thief I	
Match and Learn	63
Diglot Weave	65
Review Questions	68
The Hunter and the Thief II	
Diglot Weave	69
Story Telling	72
Word Puzzle 3	74
A Boy and His Goat I	
Scatter Chart	76
Diglot Weave	78
Review Questions	82
A Boy and His Goat II	
Diglot Weave	84
Story Telling	88
Word Puzzle 4	90
Un Sandwich dans l'Univers	
Horseshoe story	92
Scatter Chart	95
Story telling	96
Final Word Puzzle	98
Safe Return	100
Test 2	101
Answer Key	104
Recipes	105

A Note to Parents

Basic Course Objectives

The major goal of this course is to keep children excited about communicating in another language. The adventure story, the variety of activities, and the simplified teaching methods employed in the course are all designed to make learning interesting and fun.

This course is primarily for children 2nd through 4th grade. Course activities are designed specifically with these learners in mind and include matching games, story telling, speaking, drawing, creative and deductive thinking, acting, and guessing—all things which children do for fun!

Ultimately, children who complete the course can expect to understand an impressive amount of French, including common French phrases, complete French sentences, French numbers, rhymes, and questions. They will also be able to understand stories told all or mostly in French, to retell these stories themselves using French, and to make up stories of their own using words and sentence patterns they have learned.

Children who complete the course will be well prepared to continue learning with our other French courses, and they will have the foundation that will make learning at that level just as fun and interesting, albeit more challenging, as in this course.

Teaching Techniques

This course allows your children to learn by doing, to learn through enjoyable experiences. The idea is to put the experience first and the explanation after. This is important to note because it is directly opposite to how teaching—and especially foreign language teaching—is traditionally done. Typically foreign language teachers spend the majority of their time explaining complex grammar and syntax rules, and drilling students on vocabulary. In this traditional mode, rules and lists come first and experience comes last. Learning experientially, on the other hand, simulates the natural language acquisition process of children.

When children learn their native languages apparently effortlessly in early childhood, it is not through the study of grammar rules and vocabulary lists. Rather, they learn the words for things around them simply by listening to others, and they intuitively grasp an amazing amount of grammar and syntax in the same way. By using activities that simulate natural language acquisition, it is not only possible but normal for children to learn a new language quickly and enjoy doing it!

Specifically, this course motivates your children to learn French by providing learning experiences in the form of matching games, story telling exercises, drawing exercises, singing and acting, and other fun activities aimed at developing functional language comprehension and speaking ability. These activities contrast markedly with the exercises in more traditional courses, which tend to focus exclusively on learning some vocabulary, or on understanding very simple French sentences, without extending learning to the point of actually understanding and speaking the language. The language your children will acquire through this course will be more useful to them than language learned through traditional approaches, because knowledge gained in fun, rather than stressful, ways is much easier for children to retain and much more natural for them to use themselves.

Using the Course

This course is carefully designed so that it can be used either by children working primarily on their own or by parents and children working closely together. Complete instructions, simple enough to be easily followed by children, are included on the audio. Parents or other adults can enhance the course significantly by acting as facilitators: reviewing instructions, encouraging creativity and course participation, providing frequent opportunities for children to display what they have learned, rewarding effort and accomplishment, and providing enthusiasm. Keep in mind that much of the real learning takes place as you interact with your children during and after the course learning experiences.

Perhaps the most important of the above ways parents can help their children is to give them an audience for their new skills. In order to facilitate this invaluable help, we have added a new feature to the Children's Level III French Course. At the end of each activity or story we have included suggestions for a Performance Challenge. One goal of Power-Glide courses is to teach students to produce the target language creatively and independently. The new Performance Challenge feature will help children do just that. These additional exercises will increase your child's fluency, pronunciation, and confidence in the target language, as well as give you the opportunity to be directly involved in the learning process. Encourage your children to use as much French as possible and give them the audience they need to perform for. Remind your students not to worry about mistakes. Rather, encourage them to review any words they may struggle with and make sure they feel comfortable with the current material before moving to the next lesson.

Using the resources provided in the course book and on the audio, an adult learning facilitator does not need to know French or how to teach it in order to be a great learning partner. In fact, one of the most enjoyable and effective ways to learn is together, as a team.

Parents or other adults who know French can, of course, supplement the materials in this course very effectively. A proficient bilingual teacher could, for example: (1) help children learn additional vocabulary by putting several objects on table and asking and answering questions about them, such as "What is this?" or "Where is the _____?", and so on; (2) create on-the-spot diglot-weave stories by reading illustrated children's books such as Silverstein's *Are You My Mother?*, putting key words (picturable nouns) into French, and asking questions about the story or its pictures partly or completely in French; (3) involve children in making and doing things (such as making a paper airplane or finding a hidden object) giving instructions all or partly in French.

We have added another new feature to this course that will make it easier to use. For each audio track, you will see a CD icon that includes the CD number and the track number. This will help you to easily find your place from lesson to lesson.

Benefits of Second Language Acquisition

Learning a second language has many benefits. Besides the obvious value of being able to understand and communicate with others, research in the United States and Canada in the 1970s and '80s has shown that learning a second language gives children a distinct advantage in general school subject areas. Seeing linguistic and cultural contrasts as they acquire a second language, children gain insight not only into the new language and cultures, but into their own language and culture as well.

Furthermore, a considerable amount of research has shown that learning a second language in childhood helps children learn to read and write their native language. Quite possibly the best phonics training a child can receive is to learn a language like French, because French spelling is quite phonetic: when one knows French, the spelling of a French word tells him or her how to pronounce it, and (with few exceptions) the sound of a French word tells him or her how to spell it. This carries over to English and helps children intuitively understand how language works.

Our Goal

Our goal at Power-Glide is to change the way the U.S. studies language. We want to produce foreign language speakers, not just studiers. This Children's Level III French Course effectively continues the road to speaking French. We hope you and your children will find delight in the ongoing adventure of learning another language.

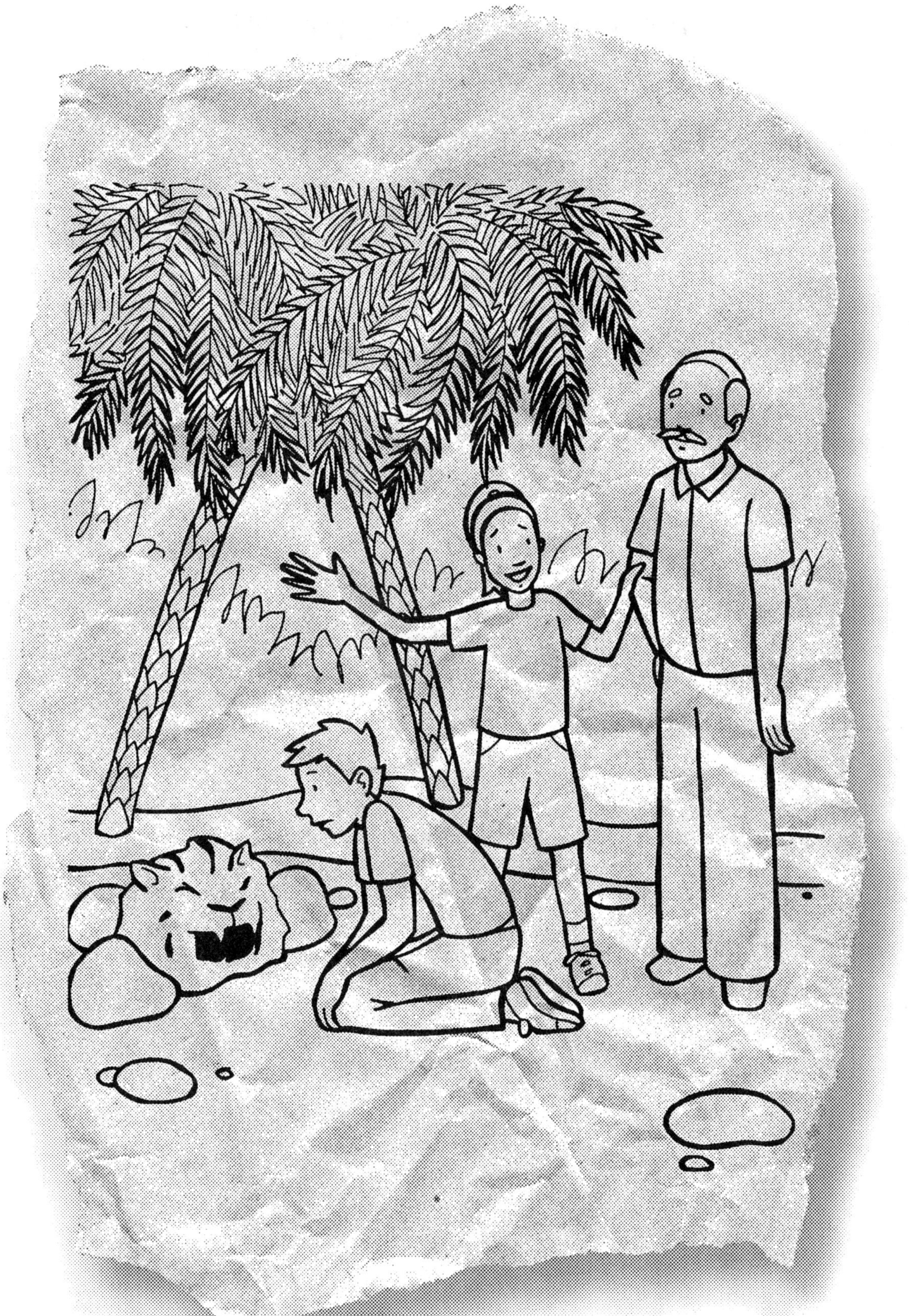

The Adventure Continues
(Martinique)

> 🔊 **Turn the audio on.**

Narrator: You are standing on the beach "Cap Chevalier" in Martinique. You have flown to Martinique, a small, French-speaking island in the Caribbean, with your Grandpa Glen, searching for a lost treasure of paintings stolen by the famous art thief Claude Revien. Your Grandpa was lucky enough to have found an old diary of Revien's and is tracing the clues. So far, your adventure has led you from your Grandpa's cottage in Marseilles, all across southern France, and through Paris. Now your Grandpa believes that the treasure might be hidden here in Martinique, where Revien escaped for his retirement.

Grandpa: This is the beach where Revien's diary said that the next clue would be hidden. Let's look around.

Lisa: What are we looking for?

Grandpa: Well, Lisa, the diary said that the next clue would be hidden "dans la dent du tigre." Do you know what that means?

Tony: "Tigre" means "tiger", I remember that.

Grandpa: That's right, Tony. "Dent" means "tooth", so "dans la dent du tigre" means "in the tiger's tooth." We need to find something that looks like a tiger.

Narrator: You begin to search the beach. The beach overlooks the Caribbean Ocean, and it is a beautiful, deep blue. It is very hot, though, and after awhile searching you begin to be discouraged.

Lisa: Tony! Look, over there. That rock, doesn't it look a little bit like a tiger's head?

Tony: You're right. Let's look closer.

Narrator: You both approach the rock, which looks exactly like a tiger with its mouth wide open.

Lisa: If the clue is in the tooth, then it would be in the mouth, right?

Tony: Yeah. We're going to have to look inside.

Narrator: Even though you know the tiger is just stone, you shiver a little bit before putting your hand inside the damp, clammy stone. You feel around and your fingers brush a piece of parchment.

Tony: I think we found it! Let's see.

Narrator: You pull out the parchment, and you see that it is, indeed, in Revien's handwriting.

Lisa: Grandpa! Grandpa! I think we found the next clue!

Grandpa: Good work children. Let me look at it. Yes, this says, Regarde dans le loup perdu—look in the Lost Wolf. Hmm. I'm not sure what this means. Let's go back to the hotel and look through Revien's diary. It might clear up where we need to go next.

Turn the audio off.

Performance Challenge:

Well you're on your way to Martinique! Find an atlas, encyclopedia, or search on the Internet to find a detailed map of Martinique. Locate the capital city and find out as much as you can about the local customs, dress, and pastimes.

Power-Glide **Children's French Level III**

Three Pigs, Chicken Little, Circus Act Mantis & the Butterfly

(Diglot Weave Review)

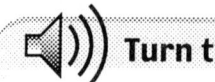

Turn the audio on.

Narrator: You and your grandpa drive back to the hotel where you have been staying in Fort-de-France, the capital city of Martinique. Fort-de-France is a fascinating, bustling city filled with palm trees and smiling people in colorful clothing. Creole music, called "zouk", is playing constantly, and you feel as if you are in the middle of a gorgeous, foreign festival. Your hotel overlooks the "Savane", a central park in the city with gardens and fountains. You can't wait to check Revien's diary to see where you get to go next.

Lisa: This is so exciting.

Grandpa: Yes it is, Lisa, but don't forget why I've allowed you and Tony to come with me. I want you to learn as much from this adventure as you can.

Tony: But, Grandpa! We have been learning!

Grandpa: Do you remember all that you've learned on this adventure, and what I taught you back at home?

Lisa: Of course we do!

Grandpa: Well, I'd like you to show me. After all, I need to be able to count on you. Tell me the story of Les trois petits cochons.

Tony: Okay... um... I can't remember it all.

Grandpa: All right, I know that was a long time ago. Let me go over some of the stories we've learned with you again, and make sure you remember them this time!

Il était une fois trois petits cochons. Les trois petits cochons are brothers, *frères*. They each built *une maison—une maison de paille, une maison de bois, et une maison de briques. Un jour, un loup* came. He went to *la maison de paille, la maison de frère numéro trois* and told *le petit cochon* to let him *entrer* or he'd *souffle et souffle* and destroy his house. *Le frère numéro trois* wouldn't let *le loup entrer*, so the wolf huffed and puffed and destroyed his *maison de paille. Le frère numéro trois s'échappé*, though, and ran to *la maison du frère numéro deux, la maison de bois. Mais le loup* came to this *maison*, too, and made the same demand. *Le frère numéro deux* wouldn't let *le loup entrer dans sa maison*, either, so *le loup* huffed and puffed and destroyed *la maison de bois.* Fortunately, *les deux petits cochons* escaped and ran to *la maison du frère numéro un, la maison de briques. Le loup* followed them but couldn't catch them, so *il* came to *la maison de briques* and knocked on *la porte* and made the same demands, but *le frère numéro un* wouldn't listen to *le loup,* either, so *le loup* huffed and puffed and puffed and huffed, and he couldn't destroy *la maison de briques. Le loup* had to go home *trés, trés affamé.*

On the way home, *le loup* sees something very strange. He sees *un éléphant se tient sur le plancher.* Then *un tigre saute sur le dos de l'éléphant. Un chien saute sur le dos du tigre. Un singe saute sur le dos du chien. Un chat saute sur le dos du singe.* Suddenly, *une souris court à travers le plancher.* Then all *les animaux* jump down *et chassent la souris. Mais la souris se sauve. La souris a de la chance!*

As it runs toward its comfortable hole in an old barn, *la souris* sees a group of animals. It sees *un poussin, une poule, un canard, un oie, un dinde, et un renard.* All *les animaux* except *le renard* are saying that *le ciel tombe. Les animaux* follow *le renard* into *sa taniére,* and none of them come back out. So *la souris* keeps running. It doesn't want *le renard* to eat it, too.

La souris stops to rest under a tree, and when it looks up, it sees another strange tableau unfolding in the tree. *Sur l'arbre, il y a une feuille. Sur la feuille, il y a un papillon. Derrière le papillon, il y a une mante. Derrière la mante, il y a un oiseau. Derrière l'oiseau, il y a un chat. Derrière le chat, il y a un serpent. Le serpent veut manger le chat. Le chat veut manger l'oiseau. L'oiseau veut manger la mante. La mante veut manger le papillon. Alors que se passe-t-il? Le papillon voit la mante et s'envole. La mante perd son repas. L'oiseau vole vers une autre branche. Le chat saute de l'arbre. Le serpent rampe au loin. La souris* was happy that the pretty *papillon s'échappé.*

Grandpa: Those are the stories you learned back in France. Be sure you remember them this time, okay?

Lisa: We will, Grandpa!

🔊 **Turn the audio off.**

Promenons-nous dans les bois
(Ditties)

Turn the audio on.

Narrator: It is close to noon when you finally arrive at your hotel, and you climb the stairs up to your room.

Grandpa: Wait. There's something wrong here.

Lisa: What is it?

Grandpa: The door is open. I closed it when we left.

Narrator: Frightened, you follow your Grandpa into the room. All of your things have been scattered around, and the chairs knocked over.

Tony: We've been robbed! This is terrible!

Grandpa: Yes, it is. Look, they found where I hid Revien's diary.

Lisa: Oh, no! We'll never find the treasure without the diary!

Tony: Wait! I bet I know who broke in. It must have been Malien! I know he still wants the treasure. Remember when he followed us into the Cathédrale Notre-Dame, Lisa, and we were so scared?

Lisa: Yes, of course. It must have been him! He's trying to find the treasure!

Grandpa: Well, if that's true, then we'll have to find the treasure without the memoirs. We can't let it fall into Malien's hands.

Tony: Do you think we'll be able to find it?

Grandpa: Well, I still have all of my folklore research, and I remember some of the things I read in the diary... yes, I think we can still do it. We'll have to work fast, though, because Malien will have the advantage. Not only does he have the memoirs, he is a native French speaker. You'll have to start learning faster than ever if we're going to keep up with him.

Lisa: Right!

Narrator: Gaining courage, you help your Grandpa search through his research looking for something that would relate to the clue, "Regarde dans le loup perdu."

Tony: Look, Grandpa, this song has the word "loup" in it.

Grandpa: Let me see... oh, yes! This is a popular children's song in French. Do you think you can learn it?

Lisa: Sure!

Grandpa: Okay. This song has ties to the fairy tale, "Little Red Riding Hood." Pay attention. First is the chorus.

> Promenons-nous dans les bois
> Pendant que le loup n'y est pas
> Si le loup y était
> Il nous mangerait
> Si le loup y est pas
> Il nous mangera pas.
>
> Loup, y es-tu! Entends-tu!
> Que fais-tu?

Now we sing a line like this:
> Je mets ma chemise.

Sing the chorus with me again.

Grandpa, Tony & Lisa:
> Promenons-nous dans les bois
> Pendant que le loup n'y est pas
> Si le loup y était
> Il nous mangerait
> Si le loup y est pas
> Il nous mangera pas.
>
> Loup, y es-tu! Entends-tu!
> Que fais-tu?

Grandpa: Good. This time we sing:
> Je mets mes chaussettes.

Grandpa, Tony & Lisa:
> Je mets mes chaussettes.

Grandpa: Good. The chorus again.

Grandpa, Tony & Lisa:
> Promenons-nous dans les bois
> Pendant que le loup n'y est pas
> Si le loup y était
> Il nous mangerait
> Si le loup y est pas
> Il nous mangera pas.

Grandpa: That's the end, so we sing:
> Et voilà!

Let's sing the whole thing again.

Grandpa, Tony & Lisa:
> Promenons-nous dans les bois
> Pendant que le loup n'y est pas
> Si le loup y était
> Il nous mangerait
> Si le loup y est pas
> Il nous mangera pas.
>
> Loup, y es-tu! Entends-tu!
> Que fais-tu?
>
> Je mets ma chemise.
>
> Promenons-nous dans les bois
> Pendant que le loup n'y est pas
> Si le loup y était
> Il nous mangerait
> Si le loup y est pas
> Il nous mangera pas.
>
> Loup, y es-tu! Entends-tu!
> Que fais-tu?
>
> Je mets mes chaussettes.
>
> Promenons-nous dans les bois
> Pendant que le loup n'y est pas
> Si le loup y était
> Il nous mangerait
> Si le loup y est pas
> Il nous mangera pas.
>
> Et voilà!

Grandpa: Excellent!

🔊 **Turn the audio off.**

Performance Challenge:

Now that you have learned a new song, share your French with a parent, friend, or one of your brothers and sisters by teaching them the song. Remember to teach it in French and then translate the words into English if your partner does not understand French. For an even greater challenge, try writing a song about your culture and put it to the tune of the French song you just learned. If you need an idea to get you started, just think of what a visitor from another country would like to know about you and your family.

J'ai perdu le do ma clarinette
(Ditties)

Turn the audio on.

Lisa: Okay. Now we now about the loup, but what about the rest of the clue?

Grandpa: Good question. Look here, though, here is another song from my research. It is called "J'ai perdu le do de ma clarinette."

Tony: Right—'perdu' like the 'loup.'

Grandpa: Exactly. Listen.
    J'ai perdu le do de ma clarinette
    J'ai perdu le do de ma clarinette.
    Ah! si Papa savait ça, tra la la,
    Il me tap'rait sur les doigts, tra la la,
    Au pas, camarade, au pas, camarade.
    Au pas, au pas, au pas.
    Au pas, camarade, au pas, camarade.
    Au pas, au pas, au pas.

The next verse in the same, but after the 'do', we add a 'ré' and a 'mi', and so on. Sing along!

Grandpa, Tony & Lisa:
    J'ai perdu le do, le ré, le mi de ma clarinette
    J'ai perdu le do, le ré, le mi de ma clarinette.
    Ah! si Papa savait ça, tra la la,
    Il me tap'rait sur les doigts, tra la la,
    Au pas, camarade, au pas, camarade.
    Au pas, au pas, au pas.
    Au pas, camarade, au pas, camarade.
    Au pas, au pas, au pas.

    J'ai perdu le do, le ré, le mi, le fa, le sol de ma clarinette
    J'ai perdu le do, le ré, le mi, le fa, le sol de ma clarinette.
    Ah! si Papa savait ça, tra la la,
    Il me tap'rait sur les doigts, tra la la,
    Au pas, camarade, au pas, camarade.
    Au pas, au pas, au pas.
    Au pas, camarade, au pas, camarade.
    Au pas, au pas, au pas.

    J'ai perdu le do, le ré, le mi, le fa, le sol, le la, le si de ma clarinette
    J'ai perdu le do, le ré, le mi, le fa, le sol, le la, le si de ma clarinette.
    Ah! si Papa savait ça, tra la la,
    Il me tap'rait sur les doigts, tra la la,
    Au pas, camarade, au pas, camarade.
    Au pas, au pas, au pas.

Au pas, camarade, au pas, camarade.
Au pas, au pas, au pas.

Grandpa: Good job!

Turn the audio off.

Performance Challenge:
Now that you have learned a new song, share your French with a parent, friend, or one of your brothers and sisters by teaching them the song. Remember to teach it in French and then translate the words into English if your partner does not understand French. For an even greater challenge, try writing a song about your culture and put it to the tune of the French song you just learned. If you need an idea to get you started, just think of what a visitor from another country would like to know about you and your family.

J'ai perdu le do ma clarinette

Power-Glide **Children's French Level III**

The Three Bears I
(Scatter Chart)

🔊 **Turn the audio on.**

Tony: Okay. Now we know that the "loup" is "perdu", but what does it mean?

Grandpa: That's a good question. I'm trying to remember, from Revien's diary, there was something about a pâtisserie that he used to go to… I think it was called Le loup perdu.

Lisa: What is a pâtisserie?

Grandpa: It's a small bakery, where they make pastries and tarts. The pâtisserie is a good example of the strong French influence on Martinique culture.

Tony: Great. Do you think the pâtisserie would still be standing?

Grandpa: I'm not sure. It would be very old. Let me make some phone calls.

Narrator: Your grandpa gets on the phone, and he begins to look for Le loup perdu. After several calls, he hangs up.

Grandpa: It looks like we're in luck. Le loup perdu is still standing, although it's been extensively renovated. Let's hope enough of the original shop is still standing to find the clue.

Narrator: You all get in the car and drive to an old little shop in downtown Fort-de-France.

Grandpa: This is it. Let's go and see what we can find.

Narrator: Inside Le loup perdu, your grandpa speaks to the owner and gets permission to search along the old walls. You begin to look over the stone, and as you search, you notice a small slip of parchment wedged in a crack.

Tony: Grandpa! Look at this!

Lisa: I think we found it!

Grandpa: Wonderful. Let's order something to eat, and we can sit down at a table outside and look this over.

Narrator: Your Grandpa orders you both some Blanc-Manger, a sweet dessert made with coconut milk. If you would like to try and make Blanc-Manger, there is a recipe in the back of your workbook. While you eat, you look over the clue.

Grandpa: This clue looks a little bit difficult. It says, "Trouvez les trois ours." I know the story that this refers to. It might be a little bit difficult.

Lisa: Well, then, we should get started.

Grandpa: You're right. Why don't we go over some of the words you're going to need to know? Listen.

Look at your workbook page, and point to what you hear.

Track 7

les trois ours
the three bears

la chambre
the bedroom

les bols
the bowls

grogna
roared

la cuisine
the kitchen

le salon
the living room

le bébé ours
the baby bear

le maman ours
the mother bear

le lit
the bed

la porte
the door

le papa ours
the father bear

la cuillére
the spoon

la chaise
the chair

quelqu'un
someone

la table
the table

la bouillie
the mush

Grandpa: Good work, children!

🔊 **Turn the audio off.**

Performance Challenge:
Choose five of the new words and pictures that you learned in the Scatter Chart. Show the pictures to a parent, friend, or one of your brothers and sisters and explain to them how you think the picture represents the words you have learned. For an even greater challenge, create your own story using the pictures. Bring out the artist in yourself by drawing your own versions of the pictographs and making a book with the story you create.

The Three Bears I — Scatter Chart

The Three Bears I
(Diglot Weave)

Turn the audio on.

Narrator: Just as you finish, you hear a voice shouting inside the pâtisserie.

Malien: Non, non! Vous ne m'aidez pas! J'ai dit, j'ai besoin de connaître quelle partie...

Tony: Do you hear that?

Lisa: It sounded like Malien!

Narrator: You sneak over to the entrance of the pâtisserie and look inside. You see a person speaking to the owner, but before you get a good look at them, they see you and quickly walk away.

Tony: Do you really think it was Malien?

Lisa: I do. He's back on the trail of the paintings!

Tony: Well, we'll just have to find them before he does.

Grandpa: That's right, Tony. We should go back the hotel. While we're on the way, let me tell you a simple version of the new story.

L'histoire de Boucle d'or et les trois ours

This is the célèbre 📖 about des trois 🐻 et Boucle d'or. As in other children's stories, cette 📖 begins with the words: il était une fois...once upon a time. Now écoute 📖.

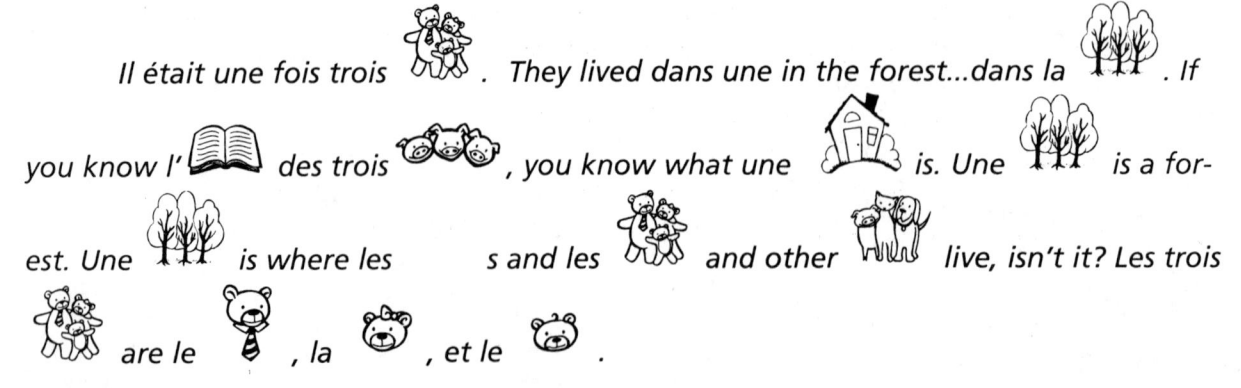

Il était une fois trois 🐻. They lived dans une in the forest...dans la 🌳. If you know l' 📖 des trois 🐷, you know what une 🏠 is. Une 🌳 is a forest. Une 🌳 is where les 🐻s and les 🐻 and other 🐕 live, isn't it? Les trois 🐻 are le 🐻, la 🐻, et le 🐻.

One morning, la 🐻 cooked up a nice pot of oatmeal 🥣. Then she set la 🪑 with trois 🥣 et trois 🥄: un grand bol et une grande 🥄 pour le

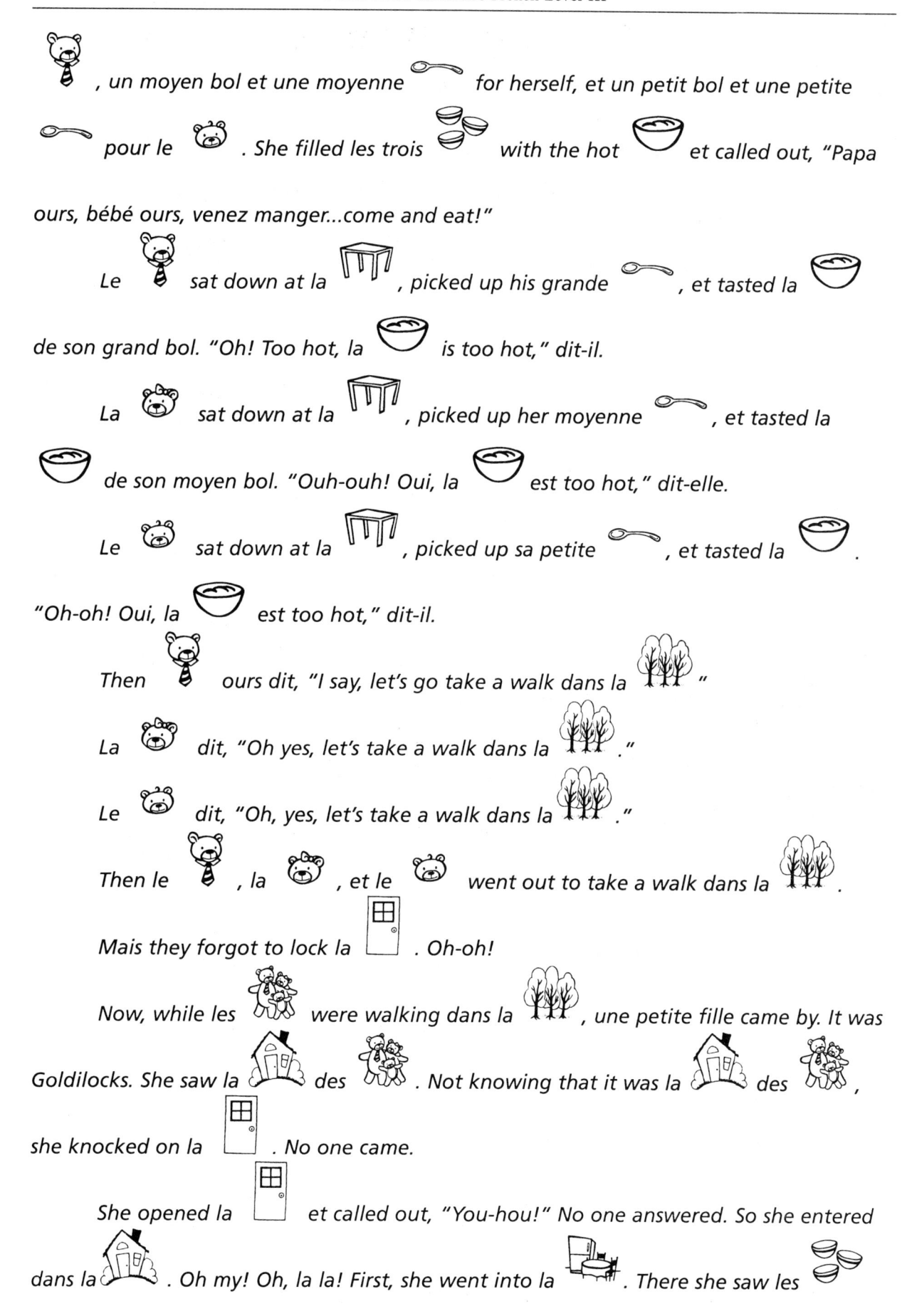

[bear] , un moyen bol et une moyenne [spoon] for herself, et un petit bol et une petite [spoon] pour le [bear] . She filled les trois [bowls] with the hot [bowl] et called out, "Papa ours, bébé ours, venez manger...come and eat!"

Le [bear] sat down at la [table] , picked up his grande [spoon] , et tasted la [bowl] de son grand bol. "Oh! Too hot, la [bowl] is too hot," dit-il.

La [bear] sat down at la [table] , picked up her moyenne [spoon] , et tasted la [bowl] de son moyen bol. "Ouh-ouh! Oui, la [bowl] est too hot," dit-elle.

Le [bear] sat down at la [table] , picked up sa petite [spoon] , et tasted la [bowl] . "Oh-oh! Oui, la [bowl] est too hot," dit-il.

Then [bear] ours dit, "I say, let's go take a walk dans la [trees] ."

La [bear] dit, "Oh yes, let's take a walk dans la [trees] ."

Le [bear] dit, "Oh, yes, let's take a walk dans la [trees] ."

Then le [bear] , la [bear] , et le [bear] went out to take a walk dans la [trees] . Mais they forgot to lock la [door] . Oh-oh!

Now, while les [bears] were walking dans la [trees] , une petite fille came by. It was Goldilocks. She saw la [house] des [bears] . Not knowing that it was la [house] des [bears] , she knocked on la [door] . No one came.

She opened la [door] et called out, "You-hou!" No one answered. So she entered dans la [house] . Oh my! Oh, la la! First, she went into la [table] . There she saw les sur la [table].

"I'm hungry," dit-elle. "J'ai faim. I think no one will mind if I taste this [bowl].

Then Goldilocks sat down at la [table], took la grande [spoon], et tasted la [bowl] du grand [bowl], le [bowl] du [bear]. "Ouh-ouh! Cette [bowl] est too hot!" dit-elle.

Then she went over et took la moyenne [spoon] et tasted la [bowl] du moyen [bowl], le [bowl] de la [bear]. "Ouh-ouh!" dit-elle. "Cette [bowl] est too hot!"

Then she went over et took la petite [spoon] et tasted la [bowl] du petit [bowl] du [bear]. "Ah!" dit-elle. "Cette [bowl] est just right." And without thinking, Goldilocks ate it all up.

Then she went into the living room...le salon. There she vit trois chaises: une grande [chair], la [chair] du [bear]; une moyenne [chair], la [chair] de la [bear] et une petite [chair], la [chair] du [bear]. First, Goldilocks sat down on la grande [chair]. "Oh! Cette [chair] est too hard," dit-elle.

Then she went over et sat down on la moyenne [chair]. "Oh! Cette [chair] est too soft," dit-elle.

Then she went over et sat down on la petite [chair], la [chair] du [bear]. "Ah! Cette [chair] est just right," dit-elle. She leaned back et CRACK! la [chair] broke. What a pity! Quel dommage!

She picked herself up and went upstairs to la chambre. There she vit trois lits: un grand lit, le [bed] du [papa bear] ; un moyen [bed], le [bed] de la [mama bear] ; et un petit [bed], le [bed] du [baby bear].

First, Goldilocks lay down on le grand [bed], le [bed] du [papa bear]. "Oh!" dit-elle. "Ce lit est too hard."

Then she went over et sat down on le moyen [bed], le [bed] de la [mama bear]. "Oh! Ce [bed] est too soft," dit-elle.

Then she went over et lay down on le petit [bed], le [bed] du bébé ours. "Ah!" dit-elle. "Ce [bed] est just right, and I am very tired." Then she laid her head on the pillow et soon fell asleep.

Just then les [bears] returned from their walk dans la [forest]. First they went into la [kitchen]. There le [papa bear] vit son bol et dit, "Oh-oh! [who] has tasted ma [soup]."

La [mama] ours vit son bol et dit, "Oh-oh! [who] has tasted ma [soup]."

Le [baby bear] vit son bol et dit, "Oh-oh! [who] has tasted ma [soup], too, and has eaten it all up." Et le [baby bear] began to cry.

Then les [bears] went into le [living room]. Le [papa bear] looked at sa grande [chair] et "ROAR!," "[who] has sat sur ma [chair]."

La [mama bear] looked at sa moyenne [chair] et dit, "[who] has sat sur ma [chair]."

Le [baby bear] looked at sa petite [chair] et dit, "[who] has sat sur ma [chair], too, and

The Three Bears I — Diglot Weave

broke it. Look!" Et le 🐻 began to cry.

Then les 🧸 went upstairs. Le 🐻 looked at son grand 🛏 et (ROAR!), "❓ has lain dans mon 🛏."

Le 🐻 looked at son moyen 🛏 et dit, "❓ has lain dans mon 🛏, also."

Le 🐻 looked at son petit 🛏 et dit, "❓ has lain dans mon 🛏, also...and HERE SHE IS!"

At that moment, Goldilocks woke up and cria, "AAAAAH!"

Then she jumped out of du 🛏 et courent hors de la 🏠 as fast as she could. Les 🧸 didn't chase after her. La 🐻 went down to la cuisine et reheated la 🥣. Le 🐻 went down to au salon et fixed la 🪑 cassée. Le 🐻 stopped crying.

And as for Goldilocks, she never walked alone dans la 🌳 after that.

🔊 **Turn the audio off.**

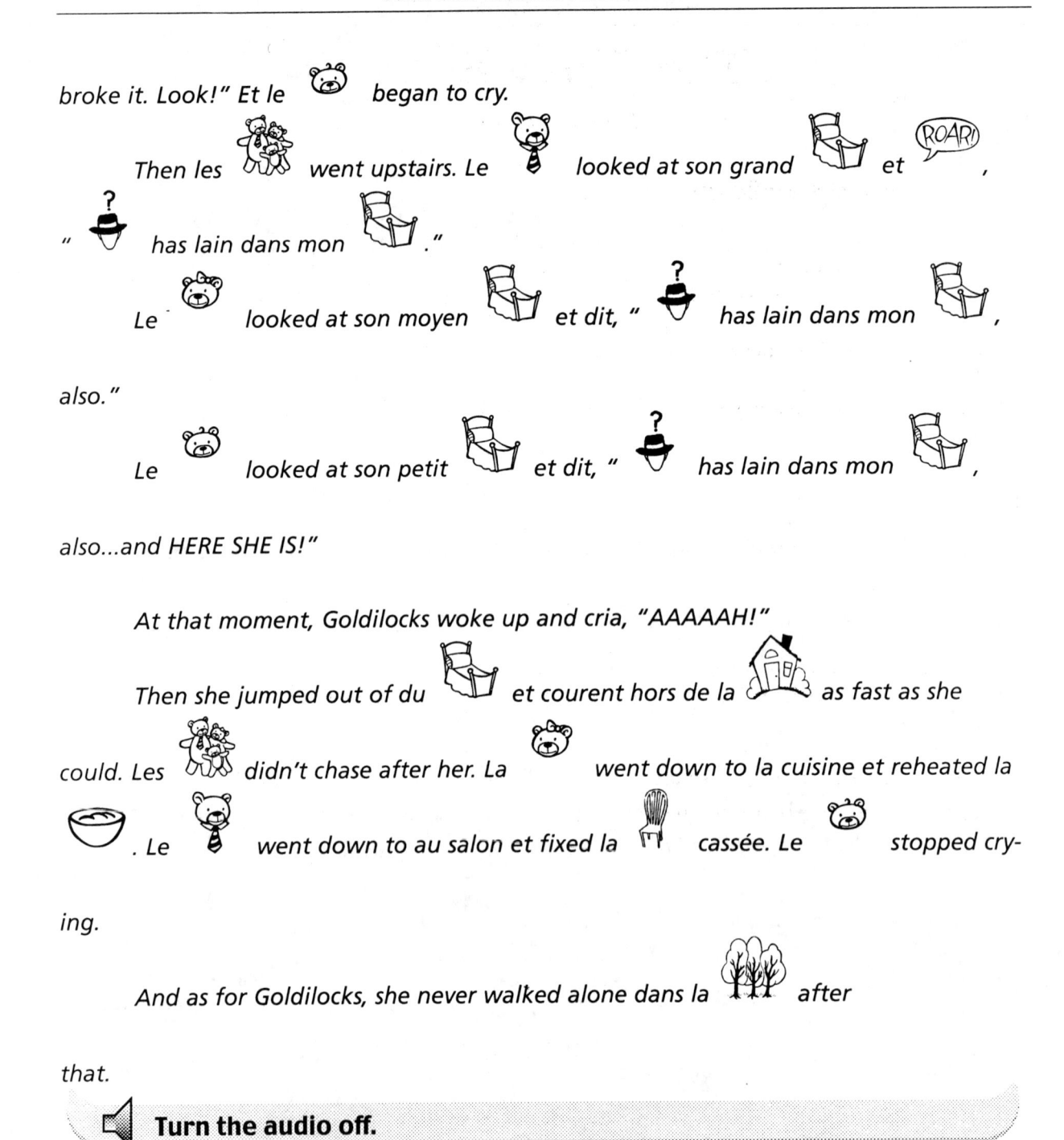

Performance Challenge:

There are four parts to this Performance Challenge:
1. Read the story silently to yourself.
2. Read the story aloud to yourself.
3. Read the story aloud to a parent, friend or one of your brothers and sisters.
4. Retell the story in your own words, using as much French as you can, to a parent, friend or one of your brothers and sisters. Don't worry if you can't remember every word. Do the best you can, and review the audio if you need to.
For an even greater challenge, write the next chapter for each diglot weave. If the story hadn't ended, what would happen next?

The Three Bears I

(Review Questions)

🔊 Turn the audio on.

Track 10

Narrator: Your grandpa is tucking you in bed, but you are too nervous to sleep. Between having the hotel room broken into and seeing Malien at the pâtisserie, you are not feeling very safe.

Lisa: Grandpa, will you stay with us until we fall asleep?

Grandpa: Yes, but you know that you don't have to worry. Nothing will happen to you as long as I'm here.

Tony: I know, but still... I want to learn how to solve the clue as fast as I can.

Grandpa: Well, let's go over what we've learned so far. Do you remember all of the story that I told you earlier?

Lisa: I think so.

Grandpa: Well, let's see if you can answer some review questions. Then, you must go to bed. Are you ready?

Note: Review questions are audio only.

🔊 Turn the audio off.

The Three Bears II
(Diglot Weave)

Turn the audio on.

Narrator: You are feeling much better by morning, and Grandpa Glen begins to pack up your bags.

Lisa: Hey, Grandpa. Are we leaving already?

Grandpa: We have no time to waste. If Malien knew enough to find Le loup perdu, he's probably figured out where to go next.

Lisa: Do we know where to go next?

Grandpa: Well, I've got a pretty good idea, but we'd better figure out as much of that puzzle as we can first. We won't have time to backtrack, just in case I'm wrong. Do you think that you are ready to learn the more advanced version of the story?

Tony: We'd better be. We don't have much time.

Grandpa: All right, then. Here's the next version.

L'histoire de Boucle d'or et les trois ours

Here is the next level of *la célèbre histoire* about *les trois ours et la petite fille* named Goldilocks. In French her *nom est Boucle d'or*. As in other children's stories, *cette histoire* begins with the words: *il était une fois*. Now *écoutez*.
Il était une fois trois ours. They lived *dans une maison dans la forêt*. If you remember the first version of *cette histoire*, you know what *une maison* is *et* what *la forêt* is. *Une forêt est* where *les loups et les ours* and other animals live, right? *Les trois ours* are *le papa ours, la maman ours, et le bébé ours*.

One morning *la maman ours* cooked up a pot of oatmeal, *bouillie*. Then she set *la table* with *trois bols et trois cuillères; un grand bol et une grande cuillère pour le papa ours, un moyen bol et une moyenne cuillère* for herself, *et un petit bol et une petite cuillère pour le bébé ours*.

She filled *les trois bols* with the hot *bouillie et appela*, "*Papa ours, bébé ours, venez manger!*"
Le papa ours sat down at *la table*, picked up his *grand cuillère et* tasted *la bouillie de son grand bol*. "Oh! Too *chaude, la bouillie est* too *chaude*," *dit-il*.
La maman ours s'assit à la table, picked up *sa moyenne cuillère*, and tasted *la bouillie de son moyen bol*. "Ouh, ouh! Oui, la bouillie est trop chaude!" *dit-elle*.
Le bébé ours s'assit à la table, picked up *sa petite cuillère, et goûta la bouil-*

lie. "Oh, oh! C'est trop chaud, la bouillie est trop chaude!" dit-il.

Then le papa ours dit, "I say, let's take a walk dans la forêt."

La maman ours dit, "Oh yes, let's take une promenade dans la forêt."

Le bébé ours dit, "Oh oui, allons faire une promenade dans la forêt."

Then le papa ours, la maman ours, et le bébé ours went out faire une promenade dans la forêt. Mais they forgot to lock la porte.

Now, while les trois ours were taking une promenade dans la forêt, une petite fille came by. It was Boucle d'or. She saw la maison des trois ours. She didn't know that it la maison des trois ours. She knocked on la porte. No one came à la porte. She opened la porte et appela, "You-hou!" No one answered. So she entered dans la maison.

First she went into la cuisine. There she saw trois bols sur la table. "I'm hungry," dit-elle. "J'ai faim. I think no one will mind if I goûte this bouillie."
Then Boucle d'or s'assit à la table, picked up la grande cuillère, et goûta la bouillie du grand bol, le bol du papa ours. "Oh, oh! Cette bouillie est trop chaude!" dit-elle.

Then she went over and picked up la moyenne cuillère et goûta la bouillie du moyen bol, le bol de la maman ours. "Ouh, ouh!" dit-elle. "Cette bouillie est trop chaude, too!"

Then she went over and picked la petite cuillère et goûta la bouillie du petit bol du bébé ours. "Aaaah!" dit-elle, "cette bouillie est just right." And without thinking, Boucle d'or ate it all up . . . elle la mangea toute.
Then she went into the living room . . . le salon. There she vit trois chaises: la grande chaise, la chaise du papa ours; la moyenne chaise, la chaise de la maman ours; et la petite chaise, la chaise du bébé ours.

First Boucle d'or s'assit sur la grande chaise. "Oh! Cette chaise est trop dure," dit-elle.

Then she went over and s'assit sur la moyenne chaise. "Oh! Cette chaise est trop molle," dit-elle.

Then she went over and s'assit sur la petite chaise. "Aaaah! Cette chaise est just right," dit-elle. As she leaned back, la chaise broke.
She picked herself up and went upstairs to la chambre. There she vit trois lits: un grand lit, le lit du papa ours; un moyen lit, le lit de la maman ours; et un petit lit, le lit du bébé ours.

First Boucle d'or s'allongea sur le grand lit, le lit du papa ours. "Oh! Ce lit est trop dur!" dit-elle.

Then she went over et s'allongea sur le moyen lit. "Oh! Ce lit est trop mou!" dit-elle.

Then she went over et s'allongea sur le petit lit. "Aaaah!, Ce lit est just right," dit-elle. Then she put her head on the pillow and soon s'endormit.

Just then les trois ours returned from their promenade dans la forêt. First they went into la cuisine. There le papa ours vit son bol et dit, "Oh-oh, somebody has tasted ma bouillie."

La maman ours regarda son bol et dit, "Oh-oh, quelqu'un has tasted ma bouillie, too."

Le bébé ours regarda son petit bol et dit, "Oh, quelqu'un a goûté á ma bouillie, too, et l'a toute mangée." Et le bébé ours began to cry.

Then les trois ours went into le salon. Le papa ours looked at sa grande chaise et grogna, "Someone has sat sur ma chaise."

La maman ours regarda sa moyenne chaise et dit, "Quelqu'un has sat sur ma chaise, too."

Le bébé ours regarda sa petite chaise et dit, "Quelqu'un s'est assis sur ma chaise, aussi, et l'a cassée!" Et le bébé ours began to pleurer.

Then les trois ours went upstairs. Le papa ours looked at son grand lit et grogna, "Quelqu'un has lain sur mon lit."

La maman ours looked at son moyen lit et dit, "Quelqu'un s'est allongé sur mon lit, aussi."

Le bébé ours looked at son petit lit et dit, "Quelqu'un s'est allongé sur mon lit, aussi, ET ELLE EST ENCORE LÁ!"

Hearing this, Boucle d'or se réveilla. Seeing les ours, elle cria, "AAAAAH!" Elle sauta du lit et courent hors de la maison.

And she never returned to la maison des trois ours again.

🔊 Turn the audio off.

Performance Challenge:
There are four parts to this Performance Challenge:
1. Read the story silently to yourself.
2. Read the story aloud to yourself.
3. Read the story aloud to a parent, friend or one of your brothers and sisters.
4. Retell the story in your own words, using as much French as you can, to a parent, friend or one of your brothers and sisters. Don't worry if you can't remember every word. Do the best you can, and review the audio if you need to.

For an even greater challenge, write the next chapter for each diglot weave. If the story hadn't ended, what would happen next?

The Three Bears II

(*Story Telling*)

Turn the audio on.

Track 13

Narrator: You drive across the hot, lush landscape of Martinique. You are traveling away from the ocean, inland. After an hour on the road, you cannot contain your excitement anymore.

Tony: Grandpa, can't you please tell us where we're going?

Grandpa: Yes, you might as well know. I first found Revien's diary at an antique sale here in Martinique. A man named Pierre, who owns a sugarcane plantation nearby, was selling it. Apparently, the plantation was owned once by a friend of Revien's, and he spent some time there. Pierre found the diary in an old trunk in the attic.

Lisa: That's interesting, Grandpa, but what does it have to do with the clue?

Grandpa: The name of the plantation was Les Trois Ours.

Tony: That's it! That must be where the next clue is hidden.

Grandpa: I hope so. Unfortunately, if Malien has the diary, then he might get there before us. It's very important that he not find that clue!

Lisa: Don't worry, Grandpa. We'll help you find it.

Grandpa: Are you sure you understood everything in the story? It's very important.

Tony: I think so.

Grandpa: Okay. What I want you to do is to tell the story back to me, using as much French as you can, so I can be sure that you know it all. Okay?

Power-Glide Children's French Level III

Now retell the story, using as much French as you can.

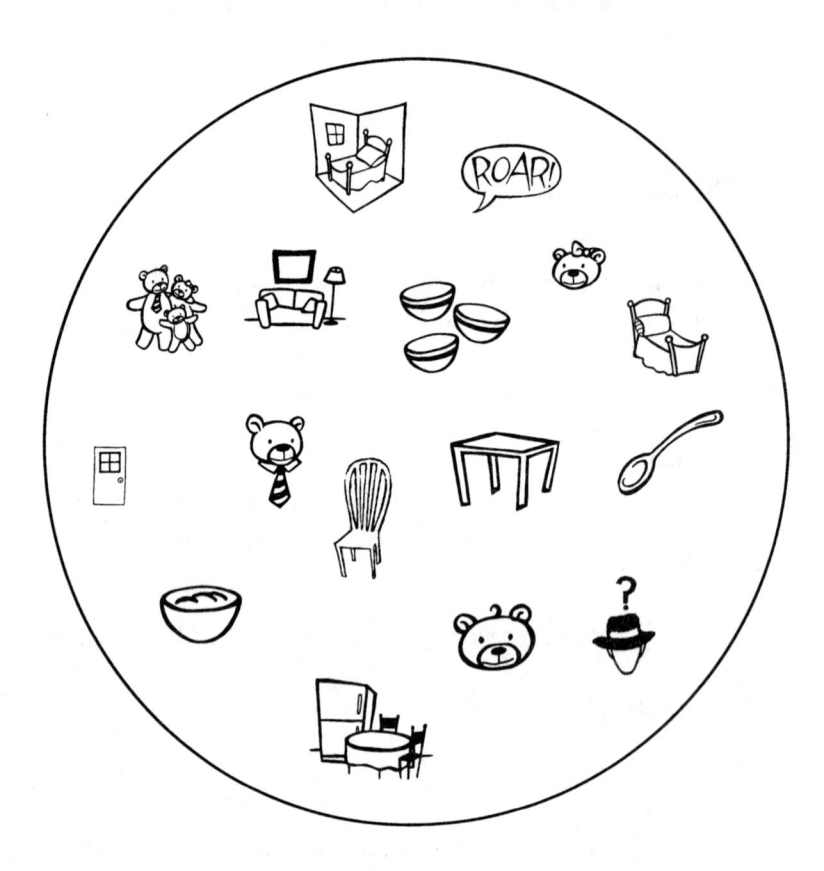

Turn the audio off.

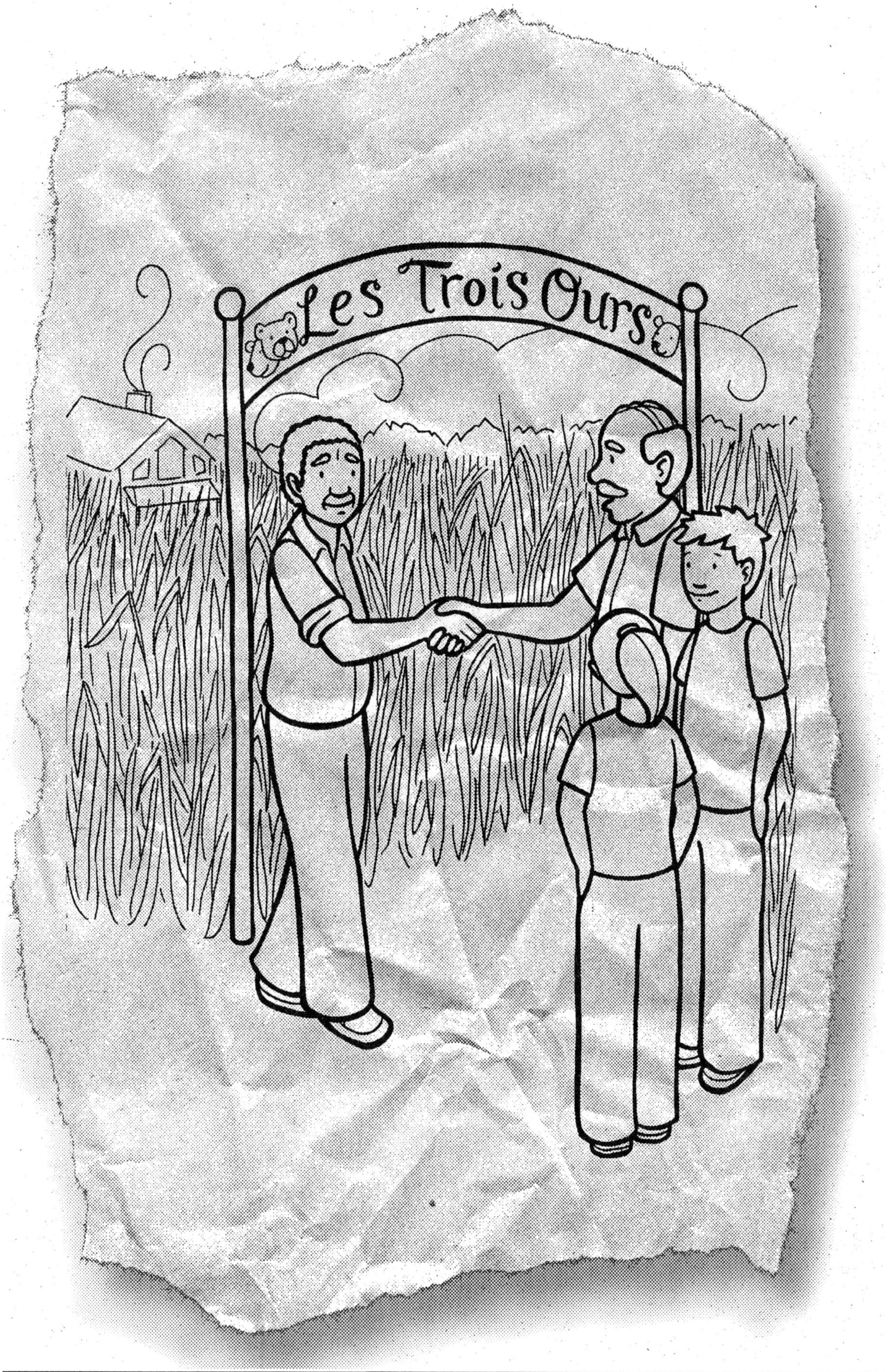
Les Trois Ours

Power-Glide **Children's French Level III**

Word Puzzle 1
(The Three Bears)

🔊 **Turn the audio on.**

Narrator: A couple of hours later you pull into a long drive that winds through fields of sugarcane. The sugarcane is tall and thin, towering feet above the car, but only about as thick as your wrist.

Tony: So, that's what sugar comes from?

Grandpa: Yes, most of the sugar in the world comes from sugarcane. It's a very big industry here in Martinique.

Narrator: You arrive at the main house of the plantation, which is enormous and white. You see a tall, strong man sitting out front wearing a straw hat against the sun. Your grandpa calls to him as you climb out of the car.

Grandpa: Pierre! Pierre, c'est moi, Glen.

Pierre: Glen! Quelle surprise! Entre.

Narrator: Pierre leads you inside his house, and offers you lemonade. As you drink, your grandpa explains to Pierre what has been going on, with the paintings and with Malien. Pierre laughs, and says he had no idea the diary would lead to so much trouble. When your Grandpa asks if he can search the plantation for the next clue, Pierre agrees and offers to help. You all go back outside and begin to wander around the outside of the house.

Lisa: The plantation's so large, Grandpa. I'm afraid we're never going to find the next clue.

Tony: Wait a minute... look, over there!

Narrator: You all run over to an old stone wall, half covered in vines, that has a mural painted on it of three bears. Pierre explains that the mural is very old, and the three bears in the painting are what the plantation was named after. You begin to search the wall, and pretty soon you find a small crack with a small piece of parchment in it.

Lisa: Is it a clue?

Grandpa: Yes. It looks like a puzzle, and you need the words from "Les trois ours." Do you think you can do it?

Tony: Well, let's see.

🔊 **Turn the audio off.**

Power-Glide **Children's French Level III**

Fill in the blanks in the puzzle below by following the numbered clues. The letters that fall in the circled blanks will make an additional word that will help you on your adventure.

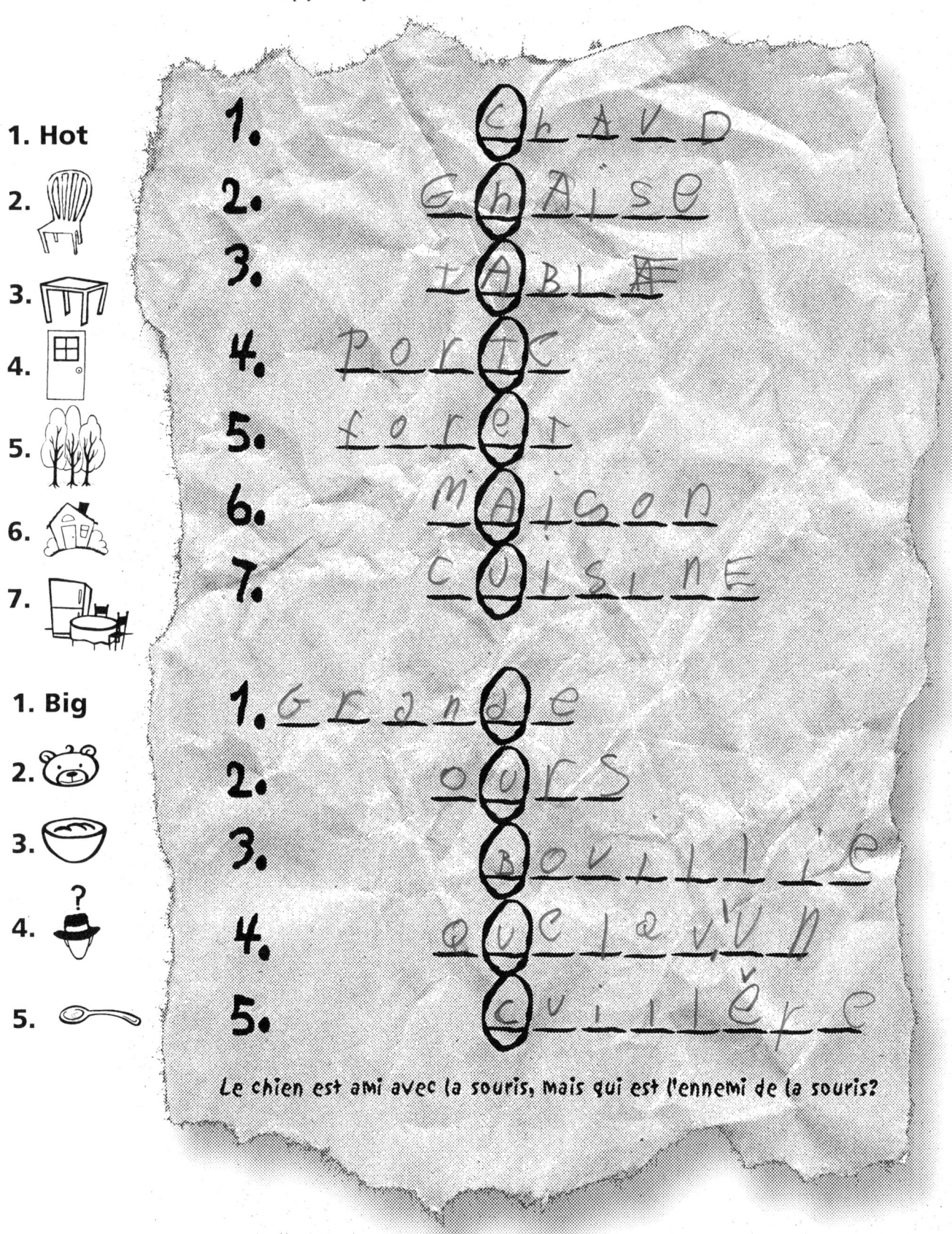

1. Hot
2. [chair]
3. [table]
4. [door]
5. [trees]
6. [house]
7. [kitchen]

1. **C**HAUD
2. **H**AISE
3. T**A**BLE
4. PO**R**TE
5. FO**R**ET
6. MA**I**SON
7. C**U**ISINE

1. Big
2. [bear]
3. [bowl]
4. [?/hat]
5. [spoon]

1. G**R**ANDE
2. **O**URS
3. B**O**UILLIE
4. QU**E**LQU'UN
5. CU**I**LLÈRE

Le chien est ami avec la souris, mais qui est l'ennemi de la souris?

Word Puzzle 1 33 The Three Bears

Power-Glide **Children's French Level III**

The Dog, the Cat, and the Mouse I
(Scatter Chart)

Turn the audio on.

Track 15

Tony: Okay. The puzzle says, "Château Dubuc." What is that?

Grandpa: The Château Dubuc is an old mansion built here in the seventeenth century. It's mostly ruins now.

Lisa: Well, that must be where the next clue is. We should go, right away!

Grandpa: You're right. But wait, look here. On the bottom of the puzzle is another clue. It says, "Le chien est ami avec la souris, mais qui est l'ennemi de la souris?"

Tony: What does that mean, Grandpa?

Grandpa: I believe it refers to a story that I remember from my folklore research. It's a little bit difficult, however. You will need to learn some new vocabulary. Okay?

Here are the words you need to learn.
Listen carefully, and point to what you hear.

Track 16

recherche — *searches*

minuit — *midnight*

le mur — *the wall*

le plancher — *the floor*

la cuisinière — *the stove*

sentir — *to smell*

bons amis — *good friends*

le trou — *the hole*

le toit — *the roof*

piéger — *to trap*

Turn the audio off.

Performance Challenge:
Choose five of the new words and pictures that you learned in the Scatter Chart. Show the pictures to a parent, friend, or one of your brothers and sisters and explain to them how you think the picture represents the words you have learned. For an even greater challenge, create your own story using the pictures. Bring out the artist in yourself by drawing your own versions of the pictographs and making a book with the story you create.

The Dog, the Cat, and the Mouse I — Scatter Chart

The Dog, the Cat, and the Mouse I
(Diglot Weave)

🔊 **Turn the audio on.**

Lisa: Okay, Grandpa. Can we hear the whole story now?

Grandpa: Well, I think that if we are going to get to the château before Malien, we need to leave. We can go over the story in the car. Pierre, merci beaucoup

Pierre: Merci.

Lisa: Oui, merci.

Pierre: De rien. Bonne chance.

Narrator: You get in the car and wave to Pierre as you leave. As you drive through the afternoon, your Grandfather tells you the next story.

Grandpa: This story is called "Chien, chat, et souris." Here is how it goes.

Une souris, un chat, et un chien vivent together under the same toit en France. They live in une maison like la maison où tu vis. Even though les animaux parlent différentes languages, le chat et le chien sont bons amis. Mais le chat n'est pas ami avec la souris. Le chat est l'ennemi numéro un. Quand le chat voit la souris, il tries to la piéger. Il wants to la manger, mais la souris s'échappe toujours. La souris court vers son hole dans le mur sous la cuisinière. There inside du hole dans le mur sous la cuisinière est lá oú vit la souris. C'est confortable et safe there. Le chat can squeeze sous la cuisinière, mais il est trop gros pour entrer dans le trou où la souris s'échappe always quand le chat tries to la piéger.

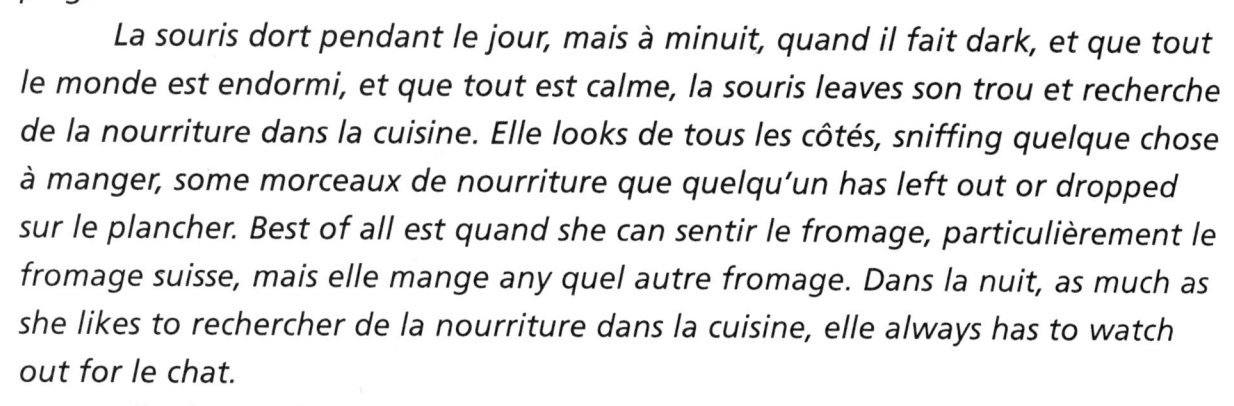

La souris dort pendant le jour, mais à minuit, quand il fait dark, et que tout le monde est endormi, et que tout est calme, la souris leaves son trou et recherche de la nourriture dans la cuisine. Elle looks de tous les côtés, sniffing quelque chose à manger, some morceaux de nourriture que quelqu'un has left out or dropped sur le plancher. Best of all est quand she can sentir le fromage, particulièrement le fromage suisse, mais elle mange any quel autre fromage. Dans la nuit, as much as she likes to rechercher de la nourriture dans la cuisine, elle always has to watch out for le chat.

Elle doesn't have to watch out au chien, parce que le chien est son ami. Even though they parlent différentes langues, ils sont bons amis. Ils sont such bons amis que parfois, quand le chien wakes up à minuit et wants to play, il goes dans la cuisine, sticks son nez sous la cuisinière et aboie softly, "arf, arf," invitant sa petite amie à sortir et play. Et la souris, knowing qu' she is safe avec le chien, sort de son trou et court çá et là dans la maison avec le chien while everyone else est endormi.

Une nuit la souris écouta to make sure que no one was awake et qu'elle could sortir de son trou et rechercher something à manger. Suddenly elle entendit a faint sound outside de son trou: "arf, arf." "Oh," elle pensa, "c'est mon ami le chien. Je vais sortir et play avec lui." Excited, elle courut hors de son trou, et le chat l'attrapa avec ses sharp claws. Le chat, qui avait attrapé la souris by la queue, saw him et dit, "arf, arf."

Now you see how useful it is to connaître another langue.
La pauvre souris thought, "If only I knew comment parler like un lion ou un chien, le chat would be scared et je could m'échapper." But la souris didn't know la langue des lions, nor la langue des chiens. Elle connaissait seulement la langue des souris.

La only thing qu'elle could dire before the end came was, "eek, eek."

🔊 **Turn the audio off.**

Performance Challenge:
There are four parts to this Performance Challenge:
1. Read the story silently to yourself.
2. Read the story aloud to yourself.
3. Read the story aloud to a parent, friend or one of your brothers and sisters.
4. Retell the story in your own words, using as much French as you can, to a parent, friend or one of your brothers and sisters. Don't worry if you can't remember every word. Do the best you can, and review the audio if you need to.

For an even greater challenge, write the next chapter for each diglot weave. If the story hadn't ended, what would happen next?

The Dog, the Cat, and the Mouse II
(Diglot Weave)

🔊 **Turn the audio on.**

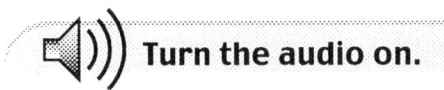

Narrator: It is mid-afternoon when you arrive at the Château Dubuc. Although it was obviously once a beautiful and imposing castle, it is now little more than a ruin. You enter the cool, dark stone building and look around.

Grandpa: Well, this is impressive. The sign outside says that the Château fell into disrepair in the eighteenth century, but they have recently restored it.

Tony: Well, we should start looking around. We want something that has to do with the riddle, "Le chien est ami avec la souris, mais qui est l'ennemi de la souris?"

Lisa: Right. Let's get going.

Narrator: You begin to wander around the Château, peering into the dark corners and stairwells, looking for the next clue.

Tony: Wait a minute, Lisa, do you hear that?

Narrator: You both get very quiet. Somewhere close by, you can hear a voice speaking to one of the curators of the Château.

Malien: Êtes-vous sûr? Je cherche une sorte de chien, ou de souris, ou de chat. Savez-vous où ils sont?

Lisa: That sounds like Malien!

Tony: I recognized some of the words he was saying, Lisa. Like chien and chat and souris.

Lisa: He must be looking for the next clue. We have to beat him to it!

Grandpa: Why are you two all huddled up? What's wrong?

Narrator: You tell your Grandpa about Malien, and he checks to see if he is still there.

Grandpa: Well, if he was here, he's gone now. He obviously hasn't found the clue yet, so we still have a chance to get it.

Tony: Tell us the whole story now, please, Grandpa?

Grandpa: Okay. Listen.

Une souris, un chat, et un chien vivent ensemble sous le même toit en France. C'est une maison comme la maison où tu vis. Même si les animaux parlent différentes langues, le chat et le chien sont bons amis.

Mais le chat n'est pas l'ami de la souris. Le chat est l'ennemi numéro un. Quand le chat voit la souris, il essaie de l'attraper. Il veut la manger, mais la souris s'échappe toujours; la souris court vers son trou dans le mur sous la cuisinière. Là, dans le trou sous la cuisinière, est là où vit la souris. C'est confortable et sûre. Le chat peut se faufiler sous la cuisinière, mais il est trop gros pour entrer dans le trou où la souris s'échappe toujours quand le chat essaie de l'attraper.

La souris dort pendant le jour, mais à minuit, quand il fait sombre et que tout le monde est endormi, et que tout est calme, la souris sort de son trou, et cherche de la nourriture dans la cuisine. Elle regarde de tous les côtés, reniflant quelque chose à manger, de la nourriture que quelqu'un a tombé sur le plancher. Le meilleur est quand elle sent le fromage, particulièrement le fromage suisse, mais elle mange n'importe quel autre fromage. Dans la nuit, la souris doit constamment faire attention au chat autant qu'elle aime renifler la nourriture dans la cuisine.

Elle n'a pas à faire attention au chien, parce que le chien est son ami, même s'ils parlent différentes langues, ils sont bons amis. Ils sont si bons amis que parfois, quand le chien se réveille au milieu de la nuit et qu'il veut jouer, il va à la cuisine, colle son nez sous la cuisinière, et aboie doucement, "ouaf, ouaf" invitant sa petite amie à sortir et à jouer. La souris, sachant qu'elle est en sûreté avec le chien, sort de son trou et court ça et là dans maison avec le chien pendant que tout le monde est endormi.

Une nuit, la souris écouta attentivement pour être sûre que personne était réveillé et qu'elle pouvait sortir de son trou, aussi chercher quelque chose à manger. Soudain, elle entendit un léger bruit à l'extérieur de son trou, "ouaf, ouaf." "Oh," elle pensa, c'est mon ami, le chien. Je vais sortir et jouer avec lui." Tout énervée, elle courut hors de son trou, et le chat l'attrapa avec ses griffes pointues. Le chat, qui avait attrapé la souris pour la queue, la regarda et dit, "ouaf, ouaf."

Maintenant vous voyez comme c'est utile de parler une autre langue. La pauvre souris pensa, "Si seulement je savais parler comme un lion ou un chien, le chat serait effrayé et je pourrai m'échapper." Mais la souris n'avait pas appris la langue des lions, ni la langue des chiens. Elle connaissait seulement la langue des souris.

La seule chose qu'elle pouvait dire avant la fin était, "couic, couic!

🔊 Turn the audio off.

Performance Challenge:
There are four parts to this Performance Challenge:
1. Read the story silently to yourself.
2. Read the story aloud to yourself.
3. Read the story aloud to a parent, friend or one of your brothers and sisters.
4. Retell the story in your own words, using as much French as you can, to a parent, friend or one of your brothers and sisters. Don't worry if you can't remember every word. Do the best you can, and review the audio if you need to.
For an even greater challenge, write the next chapter for each diglot weave. If the story hadn't ended, what would happen next?

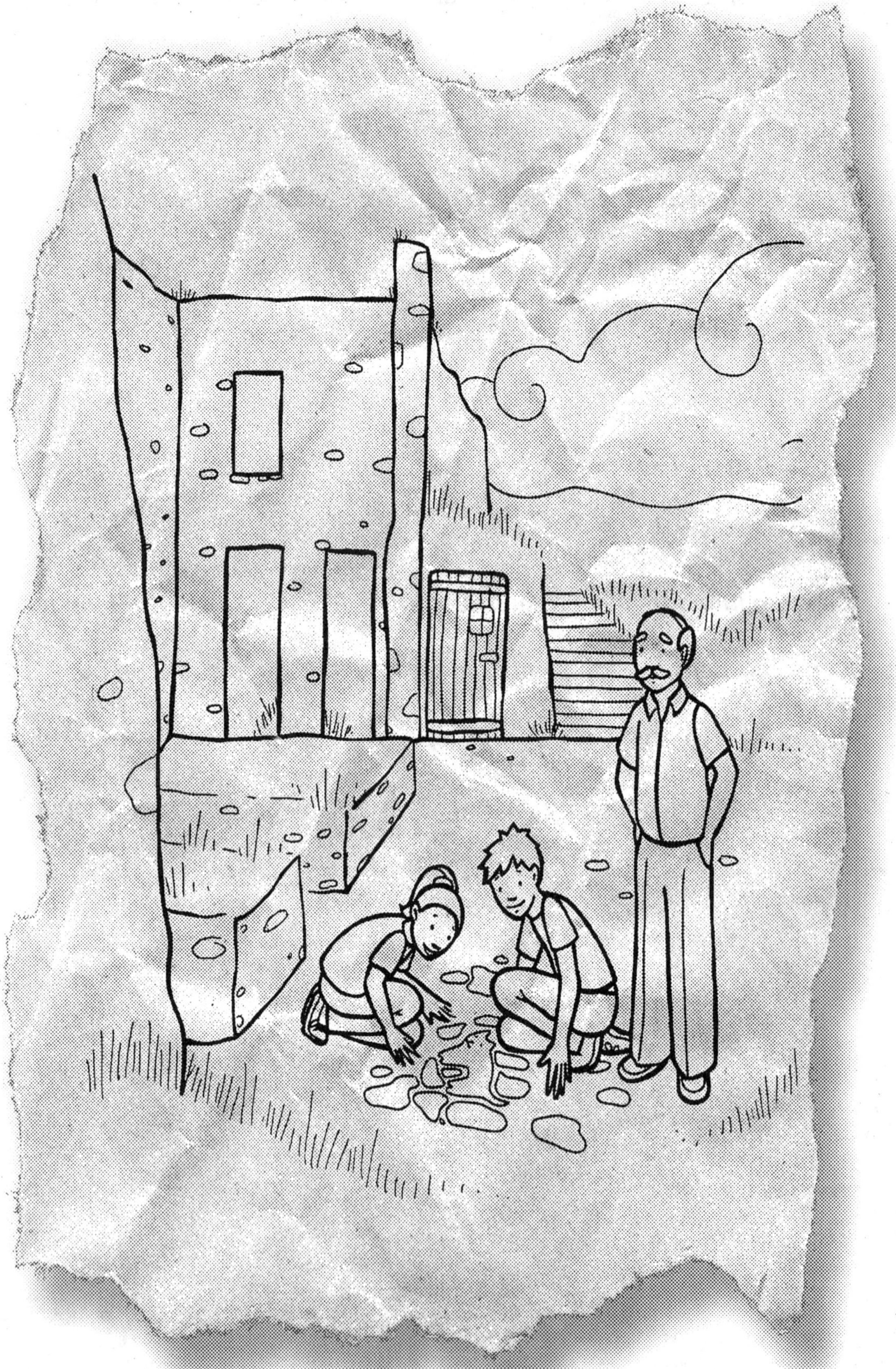

The Dog, the Cat, and the Mouse II

(Story Telling)

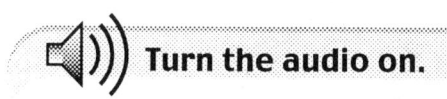

🔊 **Turn the audio on.**

Narrator: After listening to the story, you all begin to search together.

Grandpa: Okay. Let's go over our clue again and see if we can understand what it says. Le chien est ami avec la souris, mais qui est l'ennemi de la souris?

Lisa: Let's see. Le chien est ami avec la souris. That's from the story, and it means that the dog is friends with the mouse. Right?

Tony: Right. The second part of the clue is, mais qui est l'ennemi de la souris? That would be...

Lisa: The cat! Le chat.

Grandpa: Good work, children. We need to look for a chat.

Narrator: Excited, you begin to look for the cat. After awhile, however, you become discouraged.

Lisa: I'm getting tired, Tony. Let's sit down for a second.

Tony: Me too. I'm afraid we're not going to find the cat before Malien does.

Narrator: You sit down heavily on a tiled step.

Lisa: Tony, wait a minute. Look at these tiles, here.

Tony: What about them? Hey... they make a cat, don't they? This must be the cat from the clue!

Narrator: Eagerly, you both begin to look all over the tiled step.

Lisa: Tony, this tile is loose. Look, there's a little space underneath it.

Tony: And look, this must be the clue, tucked inside! But there are two pieces of parchment in here.

Lisa: Grandpa! I think we found the next clue!

Grandpa: Let me see... This first piece of paper looks like a map of some kind, but it's ripped down the middle.

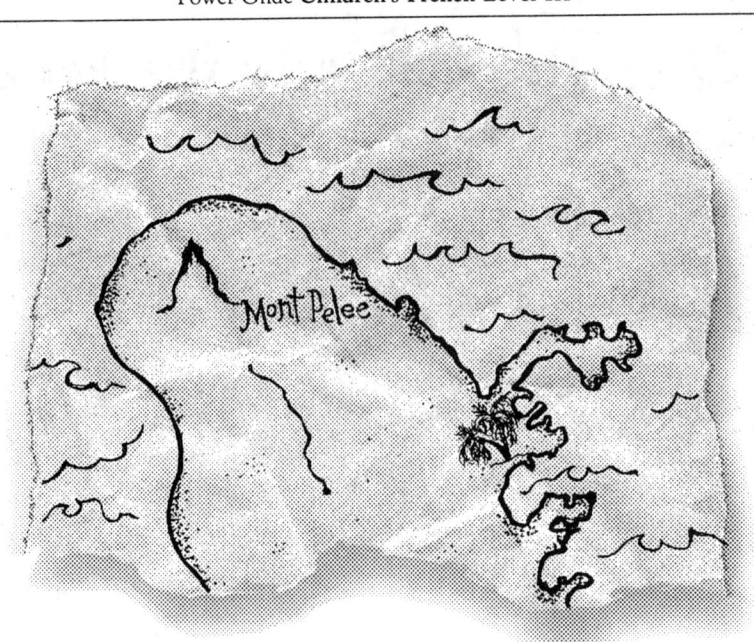

Tony: What's the other piece of paper?

Grandpa: This is another word puzzle. It looks hard. Do you think you remember all of the story well enough to do it?

Lisa: I think so.

Grandpa: Just to make sure, I want you to tell the story back to me, using as much French as you can. Make sure you remember it all!

Turn the audio off.

The Dog, the Cat and the Mouse II

Story Telling

Word Puzzle 2

(The Dog, the Cat, and the Mouse II)

Fill in the blanks in the puzzle below by following the numbered clues. The letters that fall in the circled blanks will make additional words that will help you on your adventure.

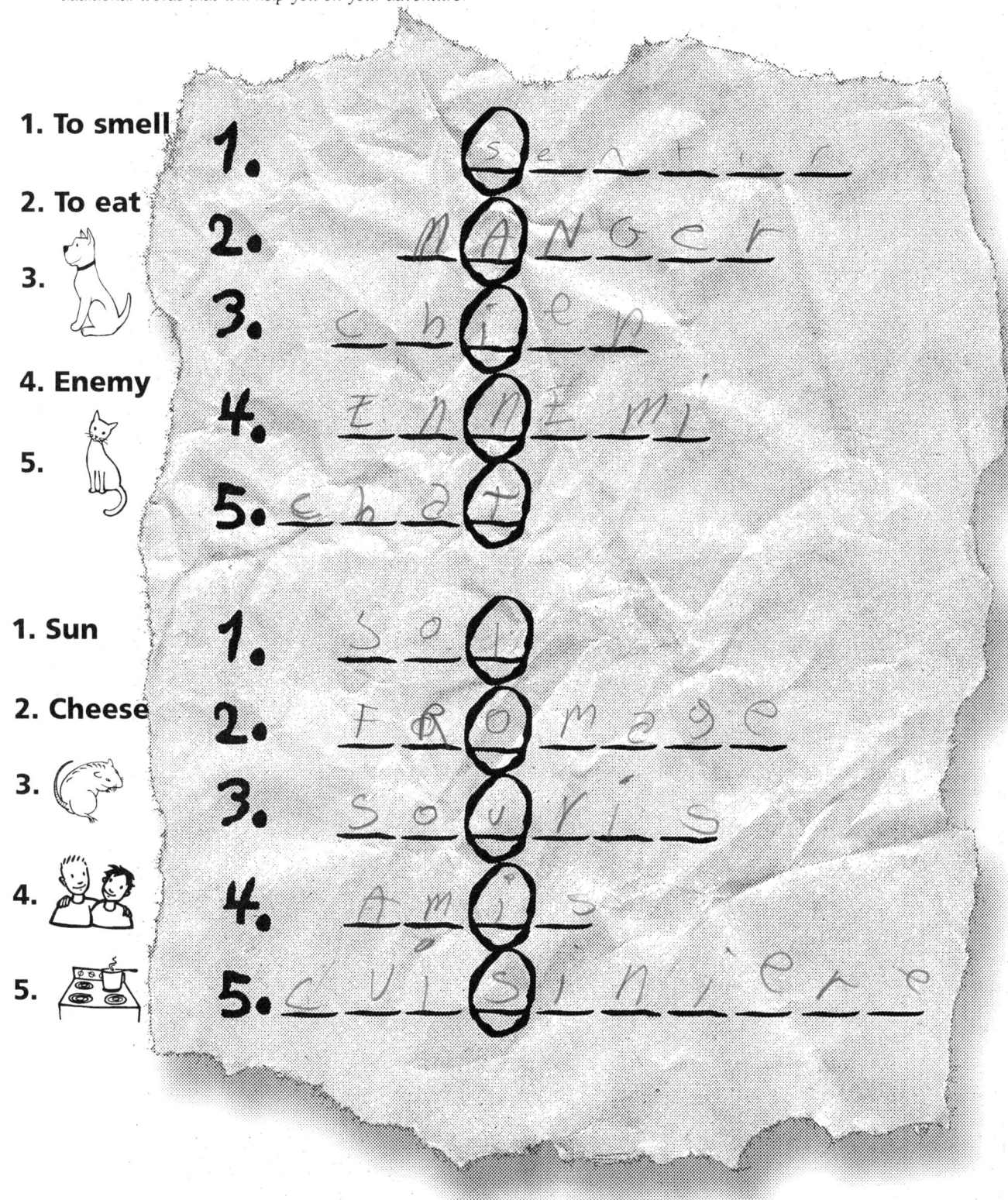

1. To smell
2. To eat
3. [dog]
4. Enemy
5. [cat]

1. s e n t i r
2. M A N G e r
3. c h i e n
4. E n n E M i
5. c h a t

1. Sun
2. Cheese
3. [mouse]
4. [friends]
5. [stove]

1. S o l
2. F r O m a g e
3. S o u r i s
4. A m i s
5. c u i s i n i e r e

Hard Days
(Horseshoe Story)

Turn the audio on.

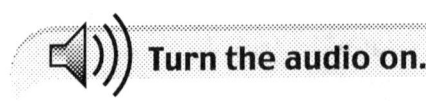

Tony: Okay. The puzzle says, "Saint Louis." What does that mean?

Grandpa: "Saint Louis" is the name of a famous fort south of Fort-de-France.

Lisa: What is a fort?

Grandpa: A fort is an army post built within walls, to protect itself during war. It comes from the French word "fort", meaning "strong." Saint Louis was built when the French settlers first came to Martinique. It was very useful when the French were under siege from the Dutch.

Tony: The next clue must be there.

Grandpa: Yes. When Revien lived on Martinique, he lived for a time inside the Saint Louis Fort. He had a small cottage he called "Jours difficiles", meaning "hard days." He called it that after one of his favorite stories. I bet that the next clue has something to do with that story.

Narrator: It is too late to head down to Fort Saint-Louis tonight, so you check into a hotel to sleep. As you get ready for bed, your Grandpa tells you the story of "Jours difficiles pour petit frère."

Tough Days for my Little Brother

1 Il y a trois jours...mon frère est tombé et s'est cassé le bras.

2 Avant hier...il s'est coupé accidentellement avec un couteau.

3 Hier...il s'est brûlé la main.

4 Aujourd'hui...il est tombé malade et s'est évanoui.

5 Demain...j'espère qu'il ira voir le docteur.

6 Après demain...je pense qu'il ira à l'hôpital.

7 Dans deux ou trois jours...j'espère qu'il sera mieux.

Turn the audio off.

Performance Challenge:
Create hand actions to represent the actions in the horseshoe story. (For example: Make up different actions to represent the animals you heard about in the story.) After you have created the actions, perform your mini-play for a parent, friend, or one of your bothers and sisters. Remember to narrate your actions in French and then translate your words if your audience does not understand French. For an even greater challenge, try writing your own horseshoe story. Choose several things or people that are related to each other in some way. Think of a chain of events that connects the characters in the story. To finish the story, figure out how the events could be reversed in order to back through the pictures and the plot.

Power-Glide Children's French Level III

Hard Days
(Scatter Chart)

🔊 **Turn the audio on.**

Track 24

Narrator: The next morning, you get up very early, before it is even light, to drive down to the Fort Saint-Louis. Yawning, you watch the sunrise from the car window.

Tony: Do you really think that we'll find the next clue before Malien does, Grandpa?

Grandpa: I hope so. Even though Malien has the diary, he doesn't have access to my folklore research, and so he doesn't know the stories that help answer the clues.

Lisa: Yeah. But, even though you told us the story, Grandpa, there are still some words that I don't understand.

Grandpa: That's a good point, Lisa. Let's go over some of the words, and make sure that you know them all.

Listen carefully and point to what you hear.

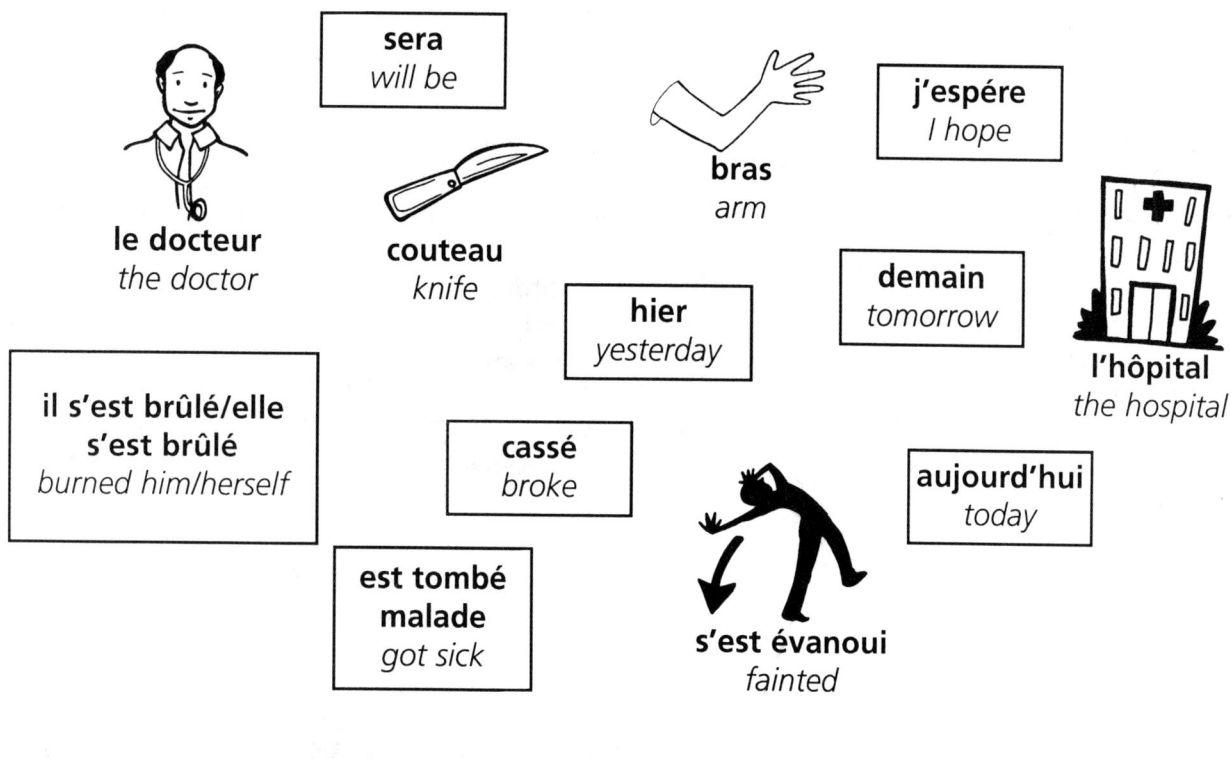

Track 25

sera — will be

le docteur — the doctor

couteau — knife

bras — arm

j'espére — I hope

demain — tomorrow

hier — yesterday

l'hôpital — the hospital

il s'est brûlé/elle s'est brûlé — burned him/herself

cassé — broke

aujourd'hui — today

est tombé malade — got sick

s'est évanoui — fainted

🔈 **Turn the audio off.**

Hard Days — Scatter Chart

Hard Days

(*Story Telling*)

🔊 **Turn the audio on.**

Narrator: You arrive at Fort Saint-Louis mid-morning. The fort is very old, surrounded by a ditch and armed with cannons. You feel as if you've stepped back in time as you enter the fort and begin to look around.

Tony: Do you remember where Revien's house would be, Grandpa?

Grandpa: I think so. Let's go and see.

Narrator: You begin to follow your Grandpa as he looks around the several small huts inside the fort.

Lisa: Look, Grandpa! There, on that hut! It still has an old sign on it, "Jours difficiles."

Grandpa: Good job, Lisa. This must be the place.

Malien: Excusez-moi, je cherche une maison appelée "Jours difficiles"...

Tony: Did you hear that?

Lisa: It's Malien! He's right over there, talking to the tour guide.

Grandpa: Quick, inside the hut!

Narrator: You duck inside "Jours difficiles" and glance around. There is almost nothing inside, except an old bed frame and a fire pit.

Tony: Where's the clue? We have to hurry, or Malien will find us!

Grandpa: Calm down. It must have something to do with the story. Okay, children, let's go over the story one more time. Tell the story back to me, using as much French as you can. Try to remember all of it!

Turn the audio off.

Hard Days — Story Telling

Mystery Maps
(Martinique)

Turn the audio on.

Tony: Wait a minute, Grandpa. One of the things that happened in the story was that il s'est brûlé la main, right?

Lisa: The fire pit! It must be in the fire pit!

Narrator: Quickly, you being searching the old pit. The pit is surrounded by heavy stones, and as you look underneath one, you find a piece of parchment.

Grandpa: This must be it. What is it?

Tony: It looks like another map, all ripped up.

Grandpa: Wait! Let's put the two ripped maps together. See? They make a map of Martinique!

Lisa: It must be showing where the paintings are hidden. How will we know where to look?

Grandpa: Well, there's directions here. Let's see if we can figure it out.

Turn the audio off.

Mont Pelee
N
Fort-de-France
St. Louis

Power-Glide Children's French Level III

Paintings!
(*Success*)

Turn the audio on.

Narrator: Armed with the map, you leave the hut and begin walking back to your car. You are nearly there when you hear a familiar voice behind you.

Malien: Attendez! Attendez! Arrêtez ces enfants!

Lisa: It's Malien!

Tony: He's seen us!

Grandpa: Quick, children, run to the car as fast as you can! We have to find those paintings, now!

Narrator: You all pile into the car and your Grandpa begins driving away, leaving an angry Malien behind you. You are so excited you can barely sit still as your Grandpa tries to drive the car as close to the place marked on the map as possible. You end up far off of the main roads, deep in jungle.

Grandpa: Okay, this is probably as good as we can do. Let's get out and look.

Narrator: You all begin to wander through the dense jungle, looking for anything out of the ordinary. You get deeper and deeper, and farther from the safety of the road.

Grandpa: Do you see anywhere where the paintings could be hidden?

Tony: Wait! Grandpa, over there!

Narrator: An ancient, towering tree stands before you, as big around as a car, and there is a large hollow in its trunk. It wouldn't seem so out of place, but the hollow has been very carefully sealed with stones and mortar.

Lisa: Do you think that the paintings could be inside there?

Grandpa: I'm not sure.

Narrator: You approach the tree. Although seemingly solid, the mortar holding the stones in place is very old and crumbling. You and your grandpa kick at it as hard as you can, and it only takes a few blows for the rocks to begin crumbling. You pull them out with your hands. Inside the tree is dark, and at first you can't see anything. As your eyes adjust to the dark, however, you notice several large, flat packages carefully wrapped in canvas. You pull them out one by one, and your grandpa peels off the canvas. Underneath are beautiful paintings, as fresh as if they were just finished. Some are only as big as your hand, showing the faces of lovely young women, and some are as large as windows, showing landscapes and still life paintings. The most beautiful of all is about the size of a book. In gentle reds and yellows, it depicts a landscape at sunset. You gaze on all the paintings in admiration.

Lisa: I can't believe it! We did it!

Tony: We found the paintings!

🔊 **Turn the audio off.**

Paintings! 51 Success

Test I
(Review)

🔊 **Turn the audio on.**

Narrator: It is now a week later. You are sitting in Grandpa's living room in Marseille, France, right where your adventure began. The newspapers and the news on TV have all carried the story of the heroes who found the stolen French paintings and returned them to the local museums. Your parents are very proud.

Tony: And do you know what the best thing is? I haven't seen Malien since this whole thing ended.

Lisa: Yeah, I guess.

Tony: What's wrong?

Lisa: I don't know. I guess I don't trust Malien. Where has he gone? He really wanted those paintings. I don't think he's going to give up.

Tony: Oh, come on. What could he possibly do now?

Narrator: Just then, your Grandpa comes into the room. You take one look at his face, and you know that something is very, very wrong.

Lisa: What happened?

Grandpa: Listen, children. This is very serious. Last night, Malien broke into the museum where the paintings were being kept and he stole that beautiful painting of the sunset. That one painting was worth more than all the rest put together.

Tony: No! Not after all of our hard work!

Grandpa: I'm afraid it's true.

Lisa: What are we going to do?

Grandpa: Well, I'm going to follow him and try to get it back. I know a man, Malien's cousin, named Jean-Paul. Malien has asked Jean-Paul to help him sneak the painting out of the country, but Jean-Paul is a good man and called to tell me. Malien thinks that Jean-Paul is still helping him, but really he's waiting for a chance to help us get the painting back. Malien told Jean-Paul that he is taking the painting to Côte d'Ivoire.

Tony: Côte d'Ivoire? Where is that?

Grandpa: It's a French-speaking country in Africa. It used to be a French colony.

Lisa: When are we going?

Grandpa: No, no. It's getting far too dangerous for you to come with me. As much as I love your help and your company, I think I should go alone.

Lisa: Grandpa, please, let us come with you! Aren't we helping enough?

Grandpa: You have been a tremendous help.

Tony: Then let us come! Besides, think how much more French we could learn if we went to another country.

Grandpa: Well...

Lisa: Please? Think of how much we have already learned!

Grandpa: Okay. If you can show your parents and me how much French you've learned, and we're impressed, I'll let you come to Côte d'Ivoire with me. But you'd better do a good job!

Turn the audio off.

Test I

Track 30

🔊 **Turn the audio on.**

A. Frame Identifications

For each question, you will see a box with pictures. You will hear a statement about one of the pictures. There will be a pause of 10 seconds to identify the picture, and then the statement will be repeated.

1.

2.

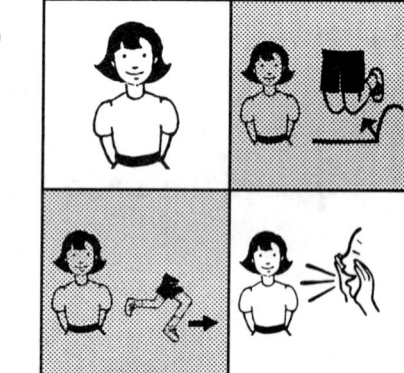

3.

4.

5.

Power-Glide Children's French Level III

Comprehension Multiple-Choice

Complete the following conversations by choosing the correct answer from the options listed.

1. "Tous ont faim."
   - A. Nous faisons une promenade dans la forêt.
   - B. Trés bien, merci.
   - C. Nous allons manger.
   - D. Oui, c'est trés sage.

2. Who owned la moyenne chaise?
   - A. La maman ours.
   - B. Le papa ours.
   - C. Le bébé ours.
   - D. Boucle d'or.

3. What was wrong with la bouillie de papa ours?
   - A. Trop mou.
   - B. Trop petite.
   - C. Trop dure.
   - D. Trop chaude

4. Why did la souris come out à minuit?
   - A. Pour jouer avec le chat.
   - B. Pour chercher quelque chose à manger.
   - C. Pour dormir dans la cuisine.
   - D. Pour sortir sa queue.

5. Quand est-ce que le docteur ira voir le petit frère?
   - A. Ça fait trois jours.
   - B. Avant-hier.
   - C. Hier.
   - D. Demain.

Now go on to complete the reading/writing portion of this test.

Turn the audio off.

Matching

Choose the statements that match and draw a line to connect the two.

1. bed — C. lit
2. stove — D. cuisinière
3. chair — B. chaise
4. bowl — E. bol
5. spoon — A. cuillère

True or False

Write T or F for each statement.

___T___ 1. Boucle d'or vit trois bols sur la table.

___F___ 2. Boucle d'or a cassée la chaise.

___F___ 3. Le chien et le chat sont ennemis.

___T___ 4. Le chat connaisssait la langue des chiens.

___F___ 5. Je n'espère pas que mon frère ira mieux.

Power-Glide Children's French Level III

Answer Key

1.

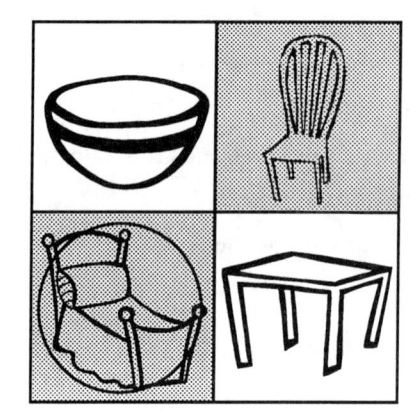

2.

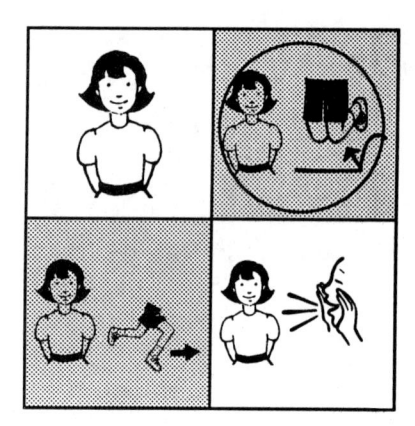

3.

4.

5.

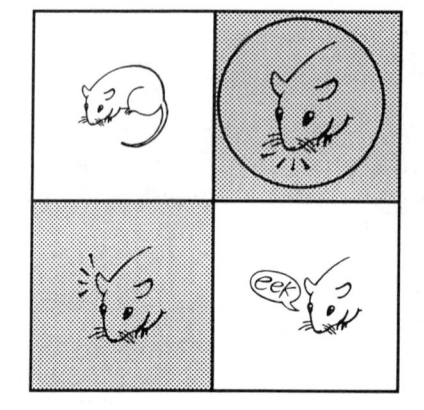

Comprehension Multiple-Choice
1. C.
2. A.
3. D.
4. B.
5. D.

Matching
1. C
2. D

3. B
4. E
5. A

True or False
1. T
2. T
3. T
4. F
5. F

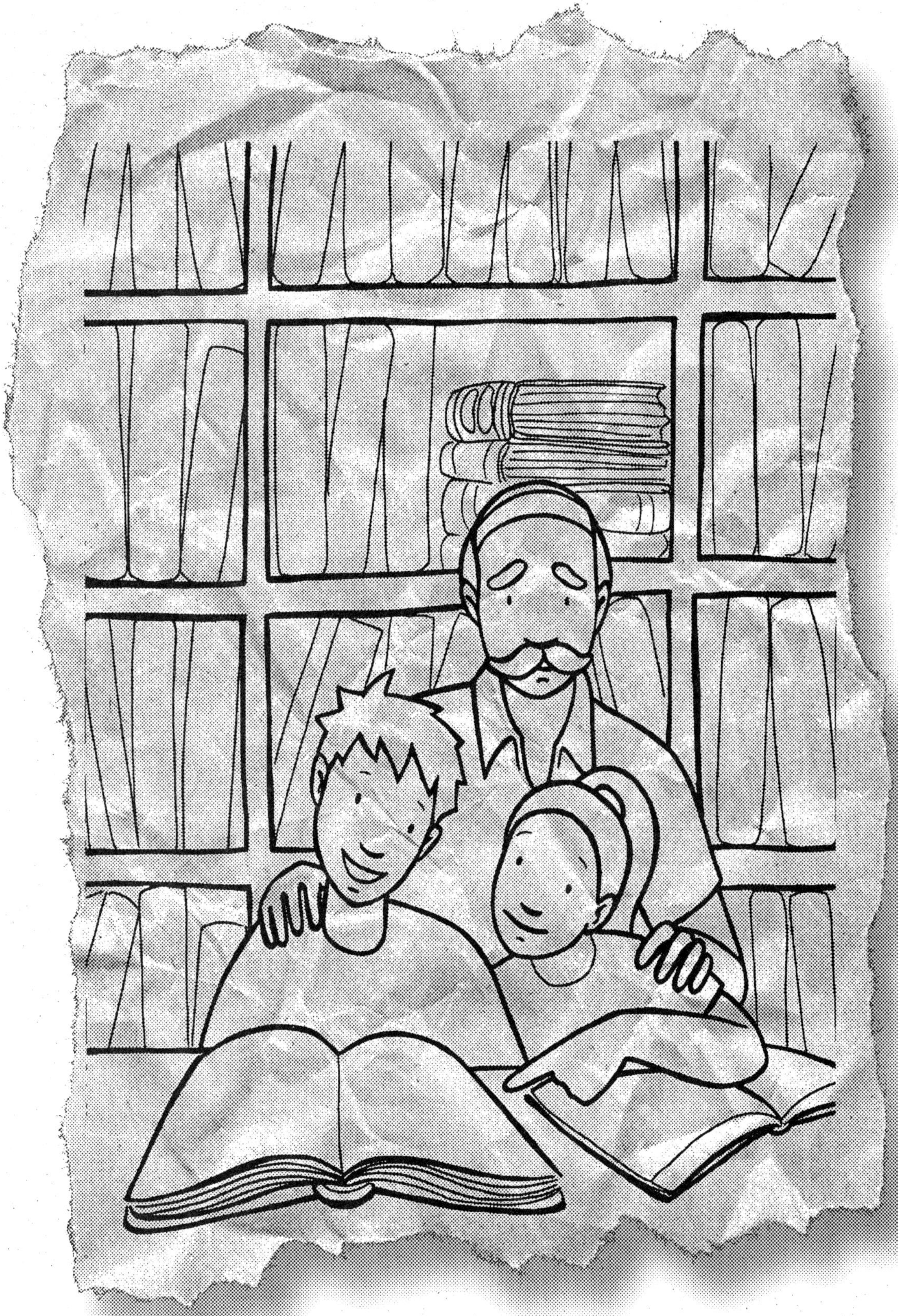

The Adventure Continues
(Côte d'Ivoire)

🔊 Turn the audio on.

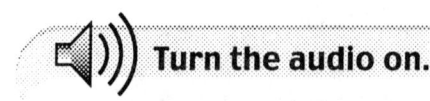

Narrator: You roll down the window of the car your grandfather has rented so that you can get a better view of Abidjan. It also lets a breeze inside, where you are stifling from the African heat. Grandpa Glen pulls the car up to your hotel, and you all hurry inside, where it is nice and cool.

Grandpa: So, what do you all think of Côte d'Ivoire?

Lisa: It's beautiful. I didn't know that any countries in Africa spoke French.

Grandpa: Oh, yes, several countries do. The French colonized parts of Africa because of the wonderful resources here--coffee, pineapple and rubber, to name a few. Now, of course, Côte d'Ivoire is its own country, but the French influence is still very strong. You'll notice that the fashions, music and food are all a unique blend of French and African traditions.

Tony: With the French traditions, Malien must have thought that he could hide out here.

Grandpa: Probably. Still, with Jean-Paul's help, I think we can find him.

Lisa: Yeah, I think so too.

Grandpa: It won't be easy. You both need to be willing to learn a lot of French and follow a lot of clues. Do you think that you can do that?

Tony: Of course we can.

Grandpa: I'm glad to hear it. While we unpack and wait for Jean-Paul to call, let's go over an exercise that I wrote to help you refresh your memories. Okay?

🔊 Turn the audio off.

Performance Challenge:
Well you're on your way to Côte d'Ivoire! Find an atlas, encyclopedia, or search on the Internet to find a detailed map of Côte d'Ivoire. Locate the capital city and find out as much as you can about the local customs, dress, and pastimes.

Fais dodo, Colas, mon petit frére
(Ditties)

🔊 **Turn the audio on.**

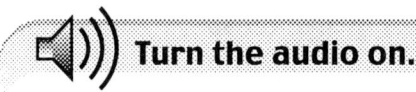

Narrator: Just then, the phone rings. Your grandpa picks it up and speaks with the other person for a moment.

Grandpa: Oui bien sûr, nous serons là.

Tony: Was that Jean-Paul, Grandpa?

Grandpa: Yes, it was. He said that he would meet us down at Le Papillon, a bookstore we both loved to come to here in Abidjan.

Lisa: Great! Let's go!

Narrator: You all run down to the car and drive to the bookstore. While most of the city is huge and swarming with people, Le Papillon is in a secluded alley. You walk inside and see aisles full of old, leather-bound books.

Grandpa: Okay. Jean-Paul is probably in here somewhere. Let's split up and look for him.

Narrator: You all begin to poke through the aisles, when you hear a voice through the shelf beside you.

Malien: Allons y. Je ne veux plus rester ici.

Tony: Lisa! Didn't that sound like Malien?

Lisa: You're right! Let's go and get Grandpa.

Narrator: You run to the other side of the store where your Grandpa is leafing through a book, and you drag him to where you heard the voice. By the time you get there, however, Malien is gone.

Tony: This is terrible! Now we'll never find them.

Grandpa: Don't worry, Tony. If I know Jean-Paul, he probably left a clue for us somewhere.

Lisa: Look, someone left a book open out here on the table. Could that be a clue?

Grandpa: Maybe. Let me see. Yes, this is a French folksong that Jean-Paul and I used in a paper we wrote together.

Tony: Will you teach it to us?

Grandpa: Yes, of course. This is a lullaby that a child is singing to his brother, Colas. Because it's a little kid's song, there are some little kid words in it. "Dodo", for instance, is how the child says "dors." It's like when you were younger, and instead of saying you were going to sleep, you said you were going "night-night."

Lisa: Oh, that's cute.

Grandpa: Exactly. Also, instead of "lait", milk, they say "lolo." Listen to the song.
    Fais dodo, Colas, mon petit frère,
    Fais dodo, t'auras du lolo.
    Maman est en haut
    Qui fait des gâteaux
    Papa est en bas
    Qui fait du chocolat.
    Fais dodo, Colas mon petit frère,
    Fais dodo, t'auras du lolo.
It's pretty easy, isn't it? Let's sing it together.

Grandpa, Tony & Lisa:
    Fais dodo, Colas, mon petit frère,
    Fais dodo, t'auras du lolo.
    Maman est en haut
    Qui fait des gâteaux
    Papa est en bas
    Qui fait du chocolat.
    Fais dodo, Colas mon petit frère,
    Fais dodo, t'auras du lolo.

Grandpa: Good. One more time.

Grandpa, Tony & Lisa:
    Fait dodo, Colas, mon petit frère,
    Fait dodo, t'auras du lolo.
    Maman est en haut
    Qui fait des gateaux
    Papa est en bas
    Qui fait du chocolat.
    Fais dodo, Colas mon petit frère,
    Fais dodo, t'auras du lolo.

Grandpa: Good job.

🔊 **Turn the audio off.**

Performance Challenge:
Now that you have learned a new song, share your French with a parent, friend, or one of your brothers and sisters by teaching them the song. Remember to teach it in French and then translate the words into English if your partner does not understand French. For an even greater challenge, try writing a song about your culture and put it to the tune of the French song you just learned. If you need an idea to get you started, just think of what a visitor from another country would like to know about you and your family.

Lundi Matin
(Ditties)

Turn the audio on.

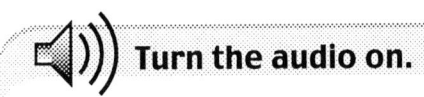

Lisa: Well, that's a neat song, Grandpa, but what could it be a clue to?

Grandpa: That's a good question, Lisa. If I had to guess, I think he'd be referring to another book we used in our study, called Mon Petit Frère. I wonder if they have it in this store.

Narrator: Your grandpa goes and asks the shopkeeper if they have the book, and the shopkeeper shows him where it is. Like the other book, it is laying out on a table, as if someone was just looking at it.

Tony: This is great, Grandpa, but how will we know where to look in the book?

Lisa: Tony! Look, there's a piece of paper stuck in between two pages.

Grandpa: You're right, Lisa. Look, it's marking the page with the song Lundi Matin. This was Jean-Paul's favorite children's song. It's a funny song about the days of the week. We'll probably need to know it to solve the next clue. Do you want to learn the song?

Tony: Yes, of course.

Grandpa: Okay. It starts with "Lundi Matin", that's Monday morning.
Lundi matin, l'empereur, sa femme et le petit prince
Sont venus chez moi pour me serrer la pince.
Comme j'étais parti
Le petit prince a dit:
"Puis c'est ainsi, nous reviendrons Mardi!"

The next verse is when they come back Mardi matin.
Mardi matin, l'emporeur, sa femme et le petit prince
Sont venus chez moi pour me serrer la pince.
Comme j'étais parti
Le petit prince a dit:
"Puis c'est ainsi, nous reviendrons Mercredi!"

The next day is "Mercredi." Sing it with me.

Grandpa, Tony & Lisa:
Mercredi matin, l'emporeur, sa femme et le petit prince
Sont venus chez moi pour me serrer la pince.
Comme j'étais parti
Le petit prince a dit:
"Puis c'est ainsi, nous reviendrons Jeudi!"

Jeudi matin, l'empereur, sa femme et le petit prince
Sont venus chez moi pour me serrer la pince.

Comme j'étais parti
Le petit prince a dit:
"Puis c'est ainsi, nous reviendrons Vendredi!"

Vendredi matin, l'emporeur, sa femme et le petit prince
Sont venus chez moi pour me serrer la pince.
Comme j'étais parti
Le petit prince a dit:
"Puis c'est ainsi, nous reviendrons Samedi!"

Samedi matin, l'empereur, sa femme et le petit prince
Sont venus chez moi pour me serrer la pince.
Comme j'étais parti
Le petit prince a dit:
"Puis c'est ainsi, nous reviendrons Dimanche!"

Grandpa: Pay attention, Dimanche is different!

Dimanche matin, l'empereur, sa femme et le petit prince
Sont venus chez moi pour me serrer la pince.
Comme je n'étais pas là,
Le petit prince se vexa:
"Puisque c'est comme ça, nous ne reviendrons pas!"

Grandpa: Excellent job.

🔊 **Turn the audio off.**

Performance Challenge:

Now that you have learned a new song, share your French with a parent, friend, or one of your brothers and sisters by teaching them the song. Remember to teach it in French and then translate the words into English if your partner does not understand French. For an even greater challenge, try writing a song about your culture and put it to the tune of the French song you just learned. If you need an idea to get you started, just think of what a visitor from another country would like to know about you and your family.

Power-Glide Children's French Level III

The Hunter and the Thief
(Match and Learn)

🔊 **Turn the audio on.**

Track 4

Lisa: What do you suppose the ditties are supposed to lead us to, Grandpa?

Tony: Well, look, Lisa. On the piece of paper that was stuck in the book, it looks like Jean-Paul wrote a clue. It says, "Rencontre-moi mercredi matin où maman faisait des gâteaux."

Grandpa: Hmmm. What could that mean?

Lisa: Well, "mercredi matin" means "wednesday morning", right? That must be when he wants to meet us.

Tony: Right. And he uses a line from the other song too... where was "Maman" making the "gâteaux"?

Lisa: "En haut." Right?

Grandpa: That's it! I forgot, Jean-Paul loved a little pâtisserie here called "Gateaux en Haut." It's right above the shop here. That must be where he wants to meet us.

Tony: Come on, let's go.

Narrator: You quickly run up the back stairs to the pâtisserie, but the store is empty except for a piece of paper lying on an empty table.

Lisa: This must be the next clue! What does it say?

Grandpa: It looks like a puzzle. Hmmm. It uses words from an old folklore story called "Le chasseur et le voleur." We'd better learn it if we're going to find out where to go next. Listen. Here are some words you're going to need to know.

Look at the pictures on your workbook page and point to what you hear.

Track 5

1.

la femme the woman	l'aigle the eagle
la nourriture the food	le voleur the thief

2.

la prison the prison	le policier the police
l'aigle the eagle	la nourriture the food

The Hunter and the Thief I   63   Match and Learn

3.

le chasseur the hunter	attrape traps
vole robs	arrête arrests

4.

avale swallows	l'aigle et le voleur the eagle & the thief
le policier et le chasseur the police & the hunter	la femme et la nourriture the woman & the food

5.

le policier arrête the police arrest	l'aigle mange the eagle eats
le voleur vole the thief robs	le chat attrape the cat traps

6.

le serpant avale the snake swallows	la souris mange la nourriture the mouse eats the food
l'aigle attaque the eagle attacks	la chasseur tue the hunter kills

7.

le voleur est en prison the thief is in prison	la femme prépare la nourriture the woman prepares the food
le chat attrape la souris the cat traps the mouse	le serpent avale le chat the snake swallows the cat

8.

l'aigle the eagle	le chasseur tue l'aigle the hunter kills the eagle
le voleur vole l'aigle the thief robs the eagle	le policier arrête le voleur the police arrest the thief

🔊 **Turn the audio off.**

Performance Challenge:

Draw a scene from the vocabulary you learned in your Match and Learn exercise. After you draw your picture, describe each part of the scene to a parent, friend, or one of your brothers and sisters. Remember to use as much French as you can to talk about your drawing. For an even greater challenge, use the different words you've learned to create sentences. You can either write the sentences or make picture sentences by drawing your own versions of the pictures from the Match and Learn activity.

The Hunter and the Thief I
(Diglot Weave)

🔊 **Turn the audio on.**

Narrator: Your grandpa is worried that he might not remember the city of Abidjan as much as he might need to, so he has called a friend of his who lives there to come and help you. You are waiting for her at a maquis, an outdoor café with tables and umbrellas in the sand. Grandpa has ordered lunch for you, a tasty chicken stew called kedjenou, which is traditionally baked in a clay pot, sealed with banana leaves and roasted in a fire. If you would like to try and make kedjenou, there is a recipe at the end of the workbook.

Tony: Does your friend speak any English, Grandpa?

Grandpa: No. Dominique was born and raised here in Abidjan, and she only speaks French. She is a naturalist, and she studies the plant and animal life in Côte d'Ivoire, and the other countries around here.

Lisa: I'm worried we won't be able to speak very well to her, if she doesn't know any English.

Grandpa: Don't worry. You two have learned a lot of French in your travels, and I think you will do just fine. While we're waiting, though, and so you can practice your French, let's go through the first version of the story. Are you ready?

C'est mon historie:
Premièrement, la femme prépare la nourriture.
Here is la femme preparing la nourriture.

Après, la souris vient et mange la nourriture.
Here is la souris eating la nourriture.

Après, le chat vient et attrape la souris.
Here is le chat catching la souris.

Après, le serpent vient et avale le chat.
Here is le serpent swallowing le chat.

Après, l'aigle vient et attaque le serpent.
Here is l'aigle falling upon le serpent.

Après, le chasseur vient et tue l'aigle.
Here is le chasseur killing l'aigle.

Après, le voleur vient et vole l'aigle.
Here is le voleur stealing l'aigle.

Après, le policier vient et arrête le voleur.
Here is le policier arresting le voleur.

Et le voleur va en prison.
Et ici, le voleur est en prison.

Poor femme! Poor souris!
Poor chat! Poor serpent!
Poor aigle! Poor chasseur!
Et poor voleur!

Turn the audio off.

Performance Challenge:
There are four parts to this Performance Challenge:
1. Read the story silently to yourself.
2. Read the story aloud to yourself.
3. Read the story aloud to a parent, friend or one of your brothers and sisters.
4. Retell the story in your own words, using as much French as you can, to a parent, friend or one of your brothers and sisters.
Don't worry if you can't remember every word. Do the best you can, and review the audio if you need to.
For an even greater challenge, write the next chapter for each diglot weave. If the story hadn't ended, what would happen next?

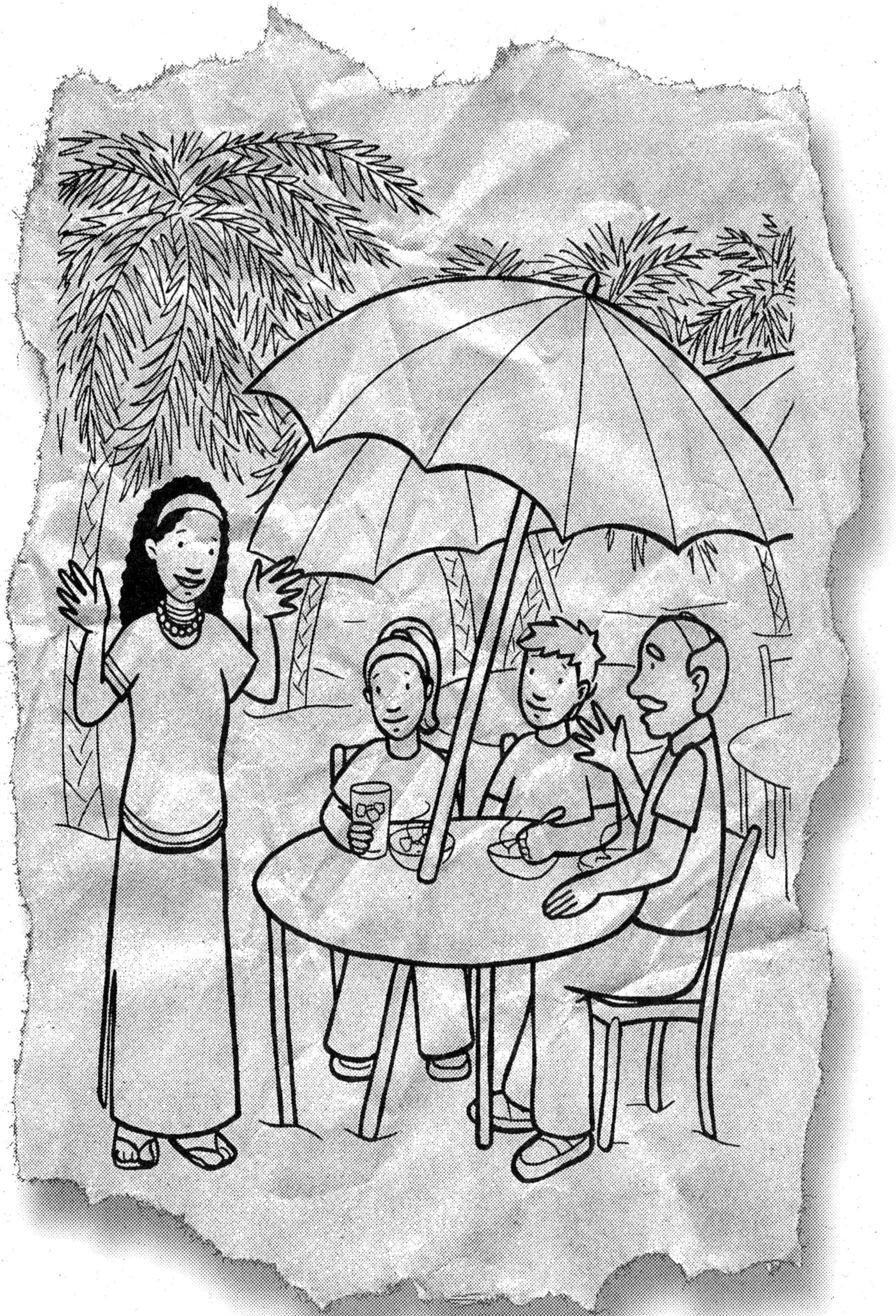

The Hunter and the Thief I
(Review Questions)

🔊 **Turn the audio on.**

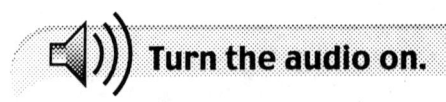

Narrator: Just then, you hear a woman's voice calling across the maquis. Dominique comes over. She is a tall, slender woman with a warm smile.

Dominique: Glen! Glen! c'est bon de vous revoir!

Grandpa: Dominique! Je suis heureux que vous soyez ici. Ils sont mes petits-enfants, Tony et Lisa.

Tony: Comment allez-vous?

Lisa: Enchantée.

Dominique: Enchantée de même.

Grandpa: Dominique offered on the phone to show us around Abidjan. Would you like to?

Tony: Yeah, that would be great.

Narrator: Dominique begins walking you all around Abidjan, showing you the interesting buildings and historical sites. Grandpa Glen fills her in on what has happened so far, and she promises to help you.

Grandpa: With Dominique's help, this hopefully won't be as difficult. Still, it's important that you understand the story I told you. Do you feel like you know it well?

Lisa: I think we understood most of it.

Grandpa: Good. Just to make sure, I'm going to ask you some questions, to see how much you understood. Okay? Same as before, you should tell me if these are vrai or faux.

Note: Review questions are audio only.

🔊 **Turn the audio off.**

The Hunter and the Thief II
(Diglot Weave)

🔊 Turn the audio on.

Dominique: Je ne connais pas l'histoire dont vous me parlez.

Grandpa: Hmmm. Dominique says she doesn't know the story of Le chasseur et le voleur.

Lisa: She'd better learn it, if she's going to help us find Malien.

Tony: Yeah. Maybe we should learn the second version of the story together.

Grandpa: Yes, I think that's a good idea. Listen carefully.

Chasseur et Voleur
Maintenant we're going to see comment you learned l'histoire.
Qu'est-ce qui s'est passé en premier?

La femme a préparé la nourriture.
Ici, la femme prépare la nourriture.

Que s'est-il passé après?
Après, une souris est venue et a mangé la nourriture.
Ici, la souris mange la nourriture.

Que s'est-il passé après?
Après, le chat est venu et a attrapé la souris.
Ici, le chat attrape la souris.

Que s'est-il passé après?
Après, le serpent est venu et a avalé le chat.
Ici, le serpent avale le chat.

Que s'est-il passé après?
Après, l'aigle est venu et a attaqué le serpent.
Ici, l'aigle attaque le serpent.

Que s'est-il passé après?

Après, le chasseur est venu et a tué l'aigle.
Ici, le chasseur tue l'aigle.

Que s'est-il passé après?
Après, le voleur est venu et a volé l'aigle.
Ici, le voleur vole l'aigle

Que s'est-il passé après?
Après, le policier est venu et a arrêté le voleur.
Ici, le policier arrête le voleur.

Que s'est-il passé après?
Le voleur est allé en prison.
Et ici, le voleur est en prison.

🔊 Turn the audio off.

Performance Challenge:
There are four parts to this Performance Challenge:
1. Read the story silently to yourself.
2. Read the story aloud to yourself.
3. Read the story aloud to a parent, friend or one of your brothers and sisters.
4. Retell the story in your own words, using as much French as you can, to a parent, friend or one of your brothers and sisters. Don't worry if you can't remember every word. Do the best you can, and review the audio if you need to.

For an even greater challenge, write the next chapter for each diglot weave. If the story hadn't ended, what would happen next?

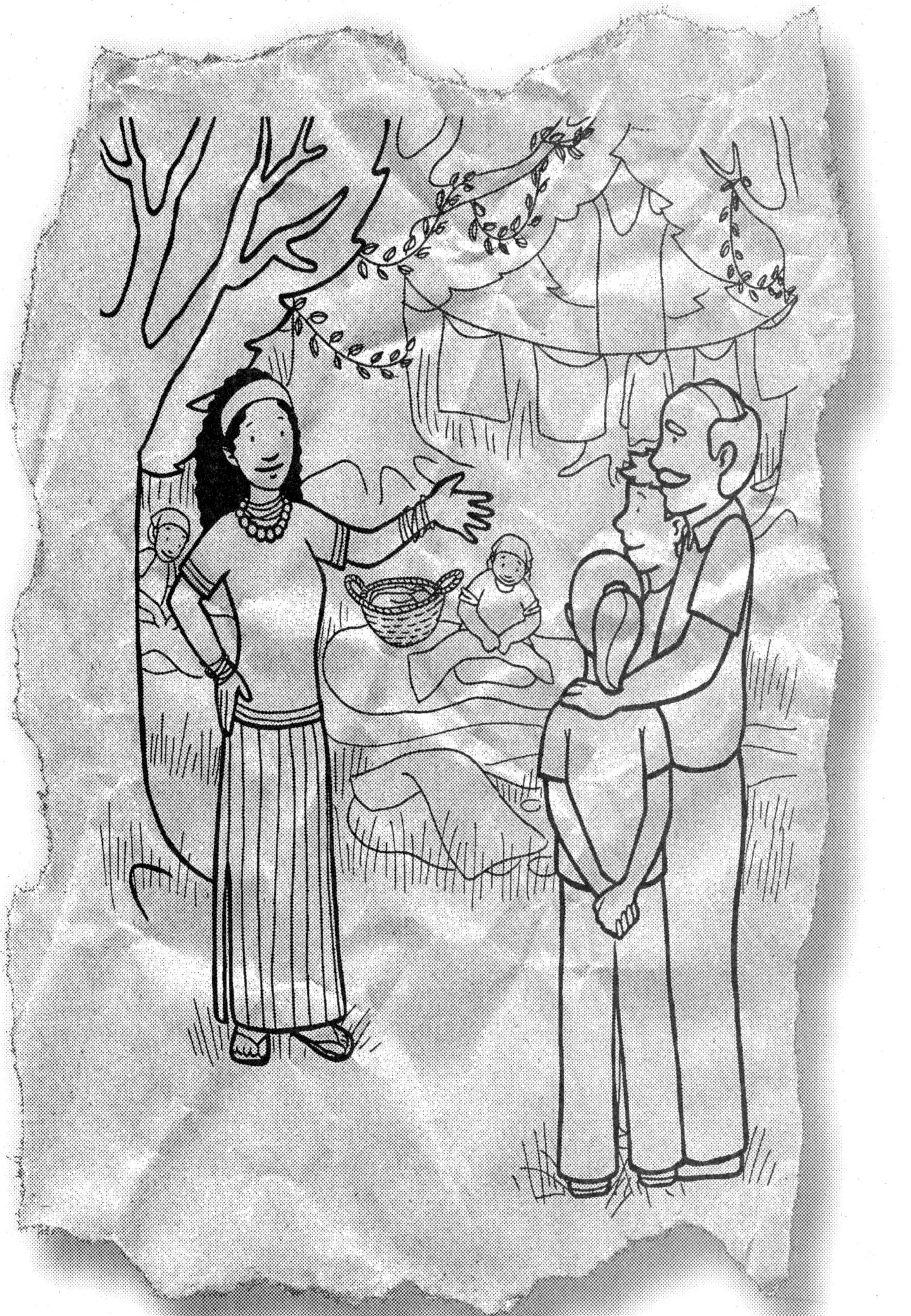

The Hunter and the Thief II
(Story Telling)

🔊 **Turn the audio on.**

Narrator: Because you expressed and interest in Dominique's naturalist work, she takes you outside of town to the Parc Du Banco, a beautiful rainforest reserve. She points out all of the exotic trees and birds that you see as you walk through the jungle. You feel as though you are in the middle of nowhere, and you are quite surprised when you stumble across hundreds of laundry workers (Dominique calls them fanicos) who are washing loads and loads of laundry in the stream that wanders through the jungle. The fanicos scrub the laundry on rocks or old tires, then spread them out to dry on the grass, so that the sea of clothing stretches out across the clearing. You sit down to watch this amazing spectacle.

Dominique: Le chasseur et le voleur est une histoire intéressante, Glen, mais combien de Français comprennent les enfants?

Grandpa: Dominique wants to know how much of my story you understood. Would you like to show her?

Lisa: Sure. I think we understood it pretty well.

Tony: Yeah. She'd be surprised at how good we are at French.

Grandpa: Okay, well, this is your chance to prove it. I want you to repeat the story back to me, using as much French as you can. Okay?

🔊 **Turn the audio off.**

Now retell the story, using as much French as you can.

- mange
- la femme
- le voleur
- arrêté
- l'aigle
- avale
- chat
- tué
- prépare
- la prison
- la nourriture
- attrapé
- vole
- le chasseur
- souris
- serpent
- policier
- attaque

Word Puzzle 3
(Story Telling)

🔊 Turn the audio on.

Dominique: Bravo, les enfants! Vous avez fait un merveilleux travail!

Tony & Lisa: Merci.

Grandpa: Dominique is right. You both learned that story very well.

Tony: Still, Grandpa, we'd better hurry if we're going to find Malien. We need to figure out that puzzle that Jean-Paul left for us.

Lisa: Yeah. Who knows where Malien might be heading next with that painting?

Grandpa: Well, I've been thinking about that. I have a theory as to why Malien would come to Côte d'Ivoire at all.

Tony: Really? Why?

Grandpa: Well, that painting is much too valuable to be sold just anywhere. Malien wanted the paintings for the money, and so he obviously won't keep it forever. I think that he has someone specific in Côte d'Ivoire that is willing to buy it from him.

Lisa: That's terrible! We'll never be able to find the painting if he sells it to someone else.

Grandpa: That's why we need to find it before he sells it. Tony is right, we need to do that puzzle, so we can find out where to go next.

🔊 Turn the audio off.

Power-Glide Children's French Level III

Fill in the blanks in the puzzle below by following the numbered clues. The letters that fall in the circled blanks will make additional words that will help you on your adventure.

1. 1. c h a t
2. Woman 2. f e m m e
3. Prison 3. p r i s o n
4. Food 4. n o u r r i t u r e
5. 5. h i s t o i r e
6. Hunter 6. c h a s s e u r
7. Police 7. p o l i c i e r
8. 8. s o u r i s
9. 9. s e r p e n t
10. Thief 10. v o l e u r

Circled letters: Y, A, M, O, R, T, E, C, I, K, P, O

Word Puzzle 3   Story Telling

A Boy and His Goat

(Scatter Chart)

Turn the audio on.

Tony: Yamoussoukro. What is that?

Dominique: Yamoussoukro est la capitale de la Côte d'Ivoire. C'est au nord.

Grandpa: Of course! The capital! Thank you, Dominique. Come on, children, we need to go immediately.

Lisa: Merci, Dominique.

Tony: Oui, merci.

Dominique: De rien. Bonne chance!

Narrator: You say goodbye to Dominique, and spend the afternoon driving to Yamoussoukro. When you enter the outskirts, you can't contain your surprise. Even though the roads are enormous, and lined with streetlights, there is almost no one outside. There are huge, towering buildings, and even a couple of lavish cathedrals, but everything seems deserted.

Tony: Where is everyone, Grandpa?

Grandpa: Well, Yamoussoukro has a very interesting history. It's actually a fairly small village, with a small population.

Lisa: A village? It's huge!

Grandpa: Well, the President of Côte d'Ivoire in the 1960's, Houphouet-Boigny, came from this town. He loved it so much, that he made it the capital, and built it into the city that you see now. The funny thing is, that it still only has the same, small number of people as before, just in a much larger space.

Narrator: You are fascinated by this strange city, and you peer around as Grandpa checks you into a hotel.

Tony: What do you think we should do now, Grandpa?

Grandpa: Well, I have an idea. The only other time I went to Yamoussoukro was when Jean-Paul and I came here to research a story. I bet it's the story he'll use in his next clue.

Lisa: We should hurry and learn it, just in case we find the next clue.

Grandpa: Good idea, Lisa. Here are some words you will need to know.

Power-Glide **Children's French Level III**

Look at the pictures on your workbook page and point to what you hear.

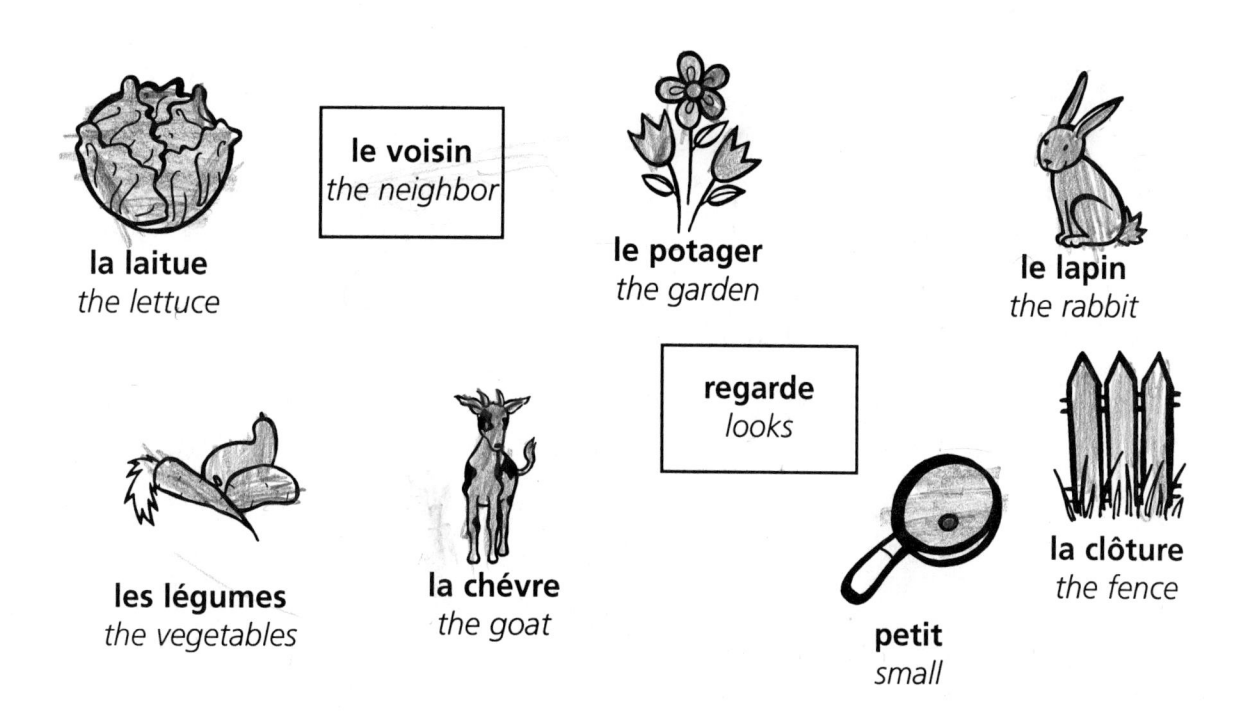

Track 14

la laitue
the lettuce

le voisin
the neighbor

le potager
the garden

le lapin
the rabbit

les légumes
the vegetables

la chévre
the goat

regarde
looks

petit
small

la clôture
the fence

🔊 **Turn the audio off.**

Performance Challenge:
Choose five of the new words and pictures that you learned in the Scatter Chart. Show the pictures to a parent, friend, or one of your brothers and sisters and explain to them how you think the picture represents the words you have learned. For an even greater challenge, create your own story using the pictures. Bring out the artist in yourself by drawing your own versions of the pictographs and making a book with the story you create.

A Boy and His Goat — Scatter Chart

Power-Glide **Children's French Level III**

A Boy and His Goat I
(Diglot Weave)

🔊 **Turn the audio on.**

Track 15

Narrator: The next morning, Grandpa takes you out into Yamoussoukro to look at the town. Despite the deserted appearance, you do see more people today, in the heart of the city. You stop outside an enormous cathedral in the middle of town, with the impressive name of Basilique de Notre Dame de la Paix, which your Grandpa says is one of the tallest churches in the world. There are dazzling stained glass windows as far up as you can see.

Tony: Well, this may not be a very big town in population, but in size it's huge. How will we ever find Malien and Jean-Paul?

Grandpa: I think our best option is to keep frequenting the places that Jean-Paul and I came together, because that's where he's most likely to meet us.

Lisa: Will you tell us the story now, the one we need to know for the next clue?

Grandpa: That's a good idea. Listen carefully.

Track 16

Un garçon et sa chèvre
Il était une fois un garçon nommé Paul. Il had a goat qui se plaisait dans le potager du voisin.

Each jour Paul went with sa chèvre au pasture près de la maison du voisin. There la chèvre ate l' sweet grass.

Et each day, as they passaient près de la maison du voisin, la chèvre looked longingly au potager.

Several fois he tried to break down la fence so he could entrer dans le potager et manger les légumes. La lettuce seemed particulièrement succulente.

Un jour as Paul led sa chèvre au pâturage, they were passaient le potager et la chévre butted la clôture avec ses horns et broke it.

Immediately la chèvre s'est mise à courir et began à manger la succulente laitue.

Paul tugged sur la rope with all ses forces. Il shouted et whistled, mais la chèvre didn't pay attention . . . ne faisait pas attention. He just kept on à manger les feuilles de la laitue.

A Boy and His Goat — 78 — Diglot Weave

De toutes ses forces Pablo tried to remove la chèvre du potager, mais he couldn't.

Alors, il s'est assis et began à pleurer.

By chance, à ce moment-là, un petit rabbit passait.

"Hé là, garçon. Pourquoi pleures-tu?"

"Je pleure parce que my chèvre a enfoncé la clôture du voison. Maintenant, elle mange les légumes, et je ne peux pas get him out. I can't even get him to raise sa tête."

"Well cela shouldn't be so difficile; I'll do it."

Le lapin a sauté vers la chèvre et a crié, "Hé, chèvre, look moi!"

Le lapin flopped ses oreilles et a sauté de haut en bas, criant, "Hé, toi! Hé, toi! Regarde-moi!"

But la chèvre didn't pay any attention. . . ne faisait pas attention. He wouldn't even lever sa tête, instead he kept on à manger la laitue.

Finally le lapin gave up et s'est assis prés de Paul, et he began à pleurer.

À ce moment-là, une renarde trottait par-là proudly, lifting sa queue high so that everyone could admire it.

"Hé, lapin, pourquoi pleures-tu?"

"Je pleure parce que la chèvre didn't pay attention to me, et le garçon pleure parce que sa chèvre a enfoncé la clôture du voisin et mange le potager, et il, can't get sa chèvre to come out."

"Bien," dit Madame Renarde, "Je ne vois any problème. So, if you don't mind, Je le ferai."

Then Madame Renarde a couru vers la chèvre and began to walk devant elle. All the time disant, "Hé chèvre, regarde-moi!"

But la chèvre ne faisait pas attention. He wouldn't even lever sa tête. He just kept à manger la laitue.

Finally Madame Renarde gave up et s'est assise et began à pleurer beside du lapin.

À ce moment-là, un grand et prideful loup passait.

"Madame Renarde, pourquoi pleurez-vous? Et pourquoi les autres pleurent?"

"Je pleure pour la même raison que le lapin, el le lapin pleure pour la même rasion que le garçon."

"Et pouquoi le garçon pleure?

"Le garçon pleure parce que sa chèvre a enfoncé la clôture du voisin et mange la laitue. Et maintenant, il ne peut pas remove la chèvre."

"Bien, je ne vois aucun problème. Je peux le faire."

Le grand loup went dans le potager et a grogné à la chèvre, "Grrrrr," and made faces à la chèvre and even s'est fâché et a soufflé.

But la chèvre ne faisait pas attention, ni même lever sa tête. He just continué à manger la laitue.

So le grand loup s'est assis et à commencé à pleurer.

Á ce moment-là, un frelon passait.

"Loup, pourquoi pleures-tu?"

"Bien, je pleure pour la même raison, que la renarde, et la renarde pleure pour la même raison que le lapin, et le lapin pleure pour la même raison que le garçon."

"Et pourquoi le garçon pleure?"

"Le garçon pleure parce que sa chèvre a enfoncé la clôture du voison et elle mange la laitue. Now he can't la chèvre to come out, ni même lui faire lever la tête."

"Bien, je ne vois aucun problème. Je peux le faire," dit le Frelon.. "Je can remove la chèvre du potager."

Á ce moment-là they all stopped de pleurer. A hornet so petit was going to la chèvre du potager? Comment could it be?

Tous watched while le frelon flew over to la chèvre. Et flew près des oreilles de la chèvre et finally he landed sur son nez.

Then le frelon a commencé to dance sur le nez de la chèvre, et cela tickled le nez de chèvre, et la chèvre began to laugh, "haa, haa. . .ha, ha," until he realized what was tickling son nez.

"UN FRELON!" La chèvre a sauté dans les airs, et le frelon stung him sur le nez, et la chèvre left le potager en courant.

Le frelon flew away, le loup slunk down la route, la renarde a trotté à travers le pâturage, et le lapin a sauté, et c'est la fin.

🔊 **Turn the audio off.**

Performance Challenge:
There are four parts to this Performance Challenge:
1. Read the story silently to yourself.
2. Read the story aloud to yourself.
3. Read the story aloud to a parent, friend or one of your brothers and sisters.
4. Retell the story in your own words, using as much French as you can, to a parent, friend or one of your brothers and sisters. Don't worry if you can't remember every word. Do the best you can, and review the audio if you need to.
For an even greater challenge, write the next chapter for each diglot weave. If the story hadn't ended, what would happen next?

Power-Glide **Children's French Level III**

A Boy and His Goat
(Review Questions)

Turn the audio on.

Track 17

Narrator: Your Grandpa is taking down a market street, which has more people buying and selling than you have seen in the rest of the city, combined. You both take an interest in all of the fascinating things there are for sale, including beautiful hand-carved wooden spoons and objects, which your Grandpa says is an art form unique to this region of the Côte d'Ivoire.

Grandpa: So, how much of the story do you feel like you understood?

Tony: Most of it, I think.

Grandpa: Good. I know that it seems like Malien has the advantage here in Côte d'Ivoire, but as long as we use our heads, I think we stand a pretty good chance of finding him and getting that painting back. To make sure that you understood the story, I'm going to ask you some review questions. Ready? Here's the first one.

Note: Review questions are audio only.

Turn the audio off.

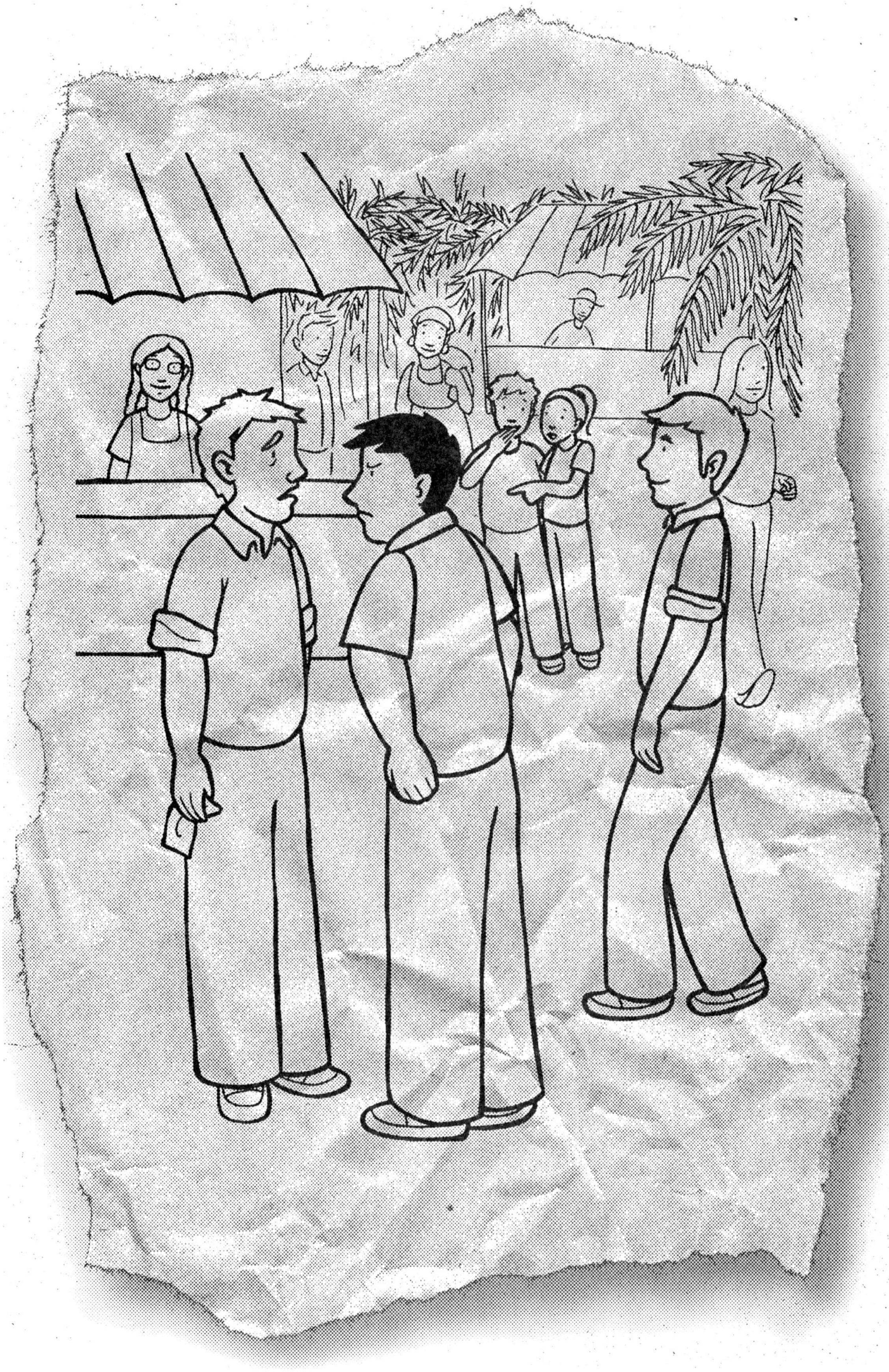

A Boy and His Goat II

(*Diglot Weave*)

Turn the audio on.

Narrator: Satisfied that you have learned the story pretty well, your Grandpa gets distracted by a booth full of clay beads and you wander a little away from him.

Tony: Do you think that we'll ever find Malien and that painting, Lisa?

Lisa: Sure, Tony. We just need to keep looking.

Narrator: Just then, you hear a familiar voice.

Malien: Venez! Allons y!

Tony: Look! Look! It's Malien!

Narrator: You duck behind the corner of a booth, and, sure enough, you see Malien standing and talking to a thin, tired looking man.

Lisa: That must be Jean-Paul.

Narrator: As if hearing his name, Jean-Paul glances up and sees you hiding behind the booth. His eyes widen. You both hold your breathe, hoping that Malien will not see you. Very carefully, you see Jean-Paul drop a piece of paper from his hand to the ground. He then follows Malien as they leave the market.

Tony: Hurry, Tony, let's go and get Grandpa!

Narrator: You run and get your Grandpa, but by the time you make it back, Malien and Jean-Paul are gone.

Grandpa: It looks like we just missed them. Did you say that Jean-Paul dropped something?

Lisa: Yes... here it is. It looks like another clue!

Grandpa: Hmmm. This looks a little bit difficult. Before we're ready to do it we should learn the second version of the story. Are you ready?

Un garçon et sa chèvre

Il était une fois un garçon nommé, Paul. Il avait une chèvre qui aimait le potager du voisin.

Chaque jour, Paul amenait sa chèvre au pâturage près de la maison du voisin.

Lá, la chèvre mangeait l'herbe.

Et chaque jour, en passant près de la maison du voisin, la chèvre regardait avec envie le potager.

Plusieurs fois, la chèvre a essayé d'enfoncer la clôture pour entrer et manger les légumes. La laitue paraissait particulièrement succulente.

Un jour, alors que Paul allait au pâturage avec sa chèvre, il passait le potager, et la chèvre enfonça la clôture avec ses cornes.

Tout de suite, la chèvre s'est mise á courir et á commencé á manger la laitue.

Paul a tiré sur la corde de toutes ses forces. Il criait et sifflait, mais la chèvre ne faisait pas attention, ni même ne levait la tête. Elle continuait simplement à manger les feuilles de la laitue.

De toutes ses forces, Paul a essayé d'éloigner la chèvre du potager, mais il ne pouvait pas.

Alors, il s'est assis et á commence á pleurer.

Par chance, á ce moment- lá, un petit lapin passait.

"Hé, garçon. Pourquoi pleures-tu ?"

"Je pleure parce que ma chèvre a enfoncé la clôture du voisin, et maintenant elle mange les légumes, et je ne peux pas la déplacer, ni même lui faire lever sa tête. "

"Bien, cela ne devrait pas être trop difficile. Je peux le faire."

Le lapin sauta sur la chèvre et a crié, "Hé, chèvre, regarde-moi ! "

Le lapin a laissé tomber ses oreilles et a sauté de haut en bas, criant, " Hé, toi! Hé toi! Regarde-moi ! "

Mais la chèvre ne faisait pas attention, ni même ne levait sa tête, elle continuait simplement à manger la laitue.

Finalement, le lapin a abandonné et s'est assis près de Paul, et a commencé á pleurer.

Á ce moment-lá, une fière renarde passait, levant sa queue si haut que tous puissent la voir.

" Hé, lapin, pourquoi pleures-tu ? "

Je pleure parce que la chèvre ne fait pas attention á moi, et le garçon pleure parce que sa chèvre a enfoncé la clôture du voisin et elle mange le potager, et il ne peut pas la déplacer.

Bien, dit Madame Renarde, je ne vois aucun problème. Alors, si vous permettez, je peux le faire.

Alors Madame Renarde a couru vers la chèvre et a commencé á marcher de long en large devant la chèvre tout en disant, "Hé, chèvre, regarde-moi. "

Mais la chèvre ne faisait pas attention ni même ne levait sa tête, elle continuait simplement à manger la laitue.

Finalement, Madame Renarde a abandonné et a commencé á pleurer près du lapin.

Á ce moment-lá, un grande et fier loup passait.

Madame Renarde, pourquoi pleurez-vous ? Et Pourquoi tout le monde pleure ?

Je pleure pour la même raison que le lapin, et le lapin pleure pour la même raison que le garçon.

Et pourquoi le garçon pleure ?

Le garçon pleure parce que sa chèvre a enfoncé la clôture du voisin et maintenant elle mange la laitue. Et il ne peut pas déplacer la chèvre, ni même lui faire lever sa tête.

Bien, je ne vois aucun problème. Je le ferai.

Le grand loup est entré dans le potager et a grogné á la chèvre, Grrrrr, et s'est fâché et a soufflé.

Mais la chèvre ne faisait pas attention, ni même ne levait sa tête, elle continuait simplement à manger la laitue.

Alors, le loup s'est assis et a commencé á pleurer.

Á ce moment-lá, un frelon passait.

"Loup, pourquoi pleures-tu ?"

"Bien, je pleure pour la même raison que la renarde, et la renarde pleure pour la même raison que le lapin, et le lapin pleure pour la même raison que le garçon."

"Et pourquoi le garçon pleure ? "

"Le garçon pleure parce que sa chèvre a enfoncé la clôture du voisin et maintenant elle mange la laitue. Et il ne peut pas la déplacer, ni même lui faire lever sa tête "

"Bien, je ne vois aucun problème. Je peux le faire,"dit le frelon. "Je peux déplacer la chèvre du potager."

Á ce moment-lá, tout le monde s'est arrêté de pleurer. "Un frelon si petit allait déplacer la chèvre du potager ? Comment cela pouvait être possible ?"

Tout le monde regardait le frelon voler au-dessus de la chèvre. Il volait, volait près des oreilles de la chèvre, et finalement atterrissait sur son nez.

Le frelon a commencé à dancé sur le nez de la chèvre, et cela a chatouillé le nez de la chèvre, et la chèvre a commencé à rire,"haa, haa. . .ha, ha," quand il a vu ce qui chatouillait son nez.

"UN FRELON!" La chèvre a sauté dans les airs, et le frelon la piqué sur le nez, et la chèvre a quitté le potager en courant.

Le frelon s'est envolé, le loup est parti par la route, la renarde a trotté à travers le pâturage, et le lapin a sauté, et c'est la fin.

🔊 **Turn the audio off.**

Performance Challenge:
There are four parts to this Performance Challenge:
1. Read the story silently to yourself.
2. Read the story aloud to yourself.
3. Read the story aloud to a parent, friend or one of your brothers and sisters.
4. Retell the story in your own words, using as much French as you can, to a parent, friend or one of your brothers and sisters. Don't worry if you can't remember every word. Do the best you can, and review the audio if you need to.
For an even greater challenge, write the next chapter for each diglot weave. If the story hadn't ended, what would happen next?

A Boy and His Goat II
(Story Telling)

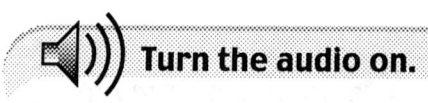

🔊 Turn the audio on.

Narrator: Eager to solve the puzzle and be on your way, you begin to hurry back to your hotel. However, night is falling and your Grandpa decides it is too late for any more adventures tonight. You are disappointed, but still very tired, as you get ready for bed.

Tony: Well, at least we know we're on the right track.

Lisa: Yeah, we almost had Malien today, and he still doesn't even know that we're after him.

Grandpa: That's true, but 'almost' won't be enough to get that painting back. Next time we are that close, I hope we really get him.

Tony: Yeah. For right now, though, we need to focus on the story.

Grandpa: Exactly. Do you think you understood it?

Lisa: I think so.

Grandpa: Okay, then, before you fall asleep, I want you to tell the story back to me, using all the French you can remember. Okay?

🔊 Turn the audio off.

Now retell the story using as much French as you can.

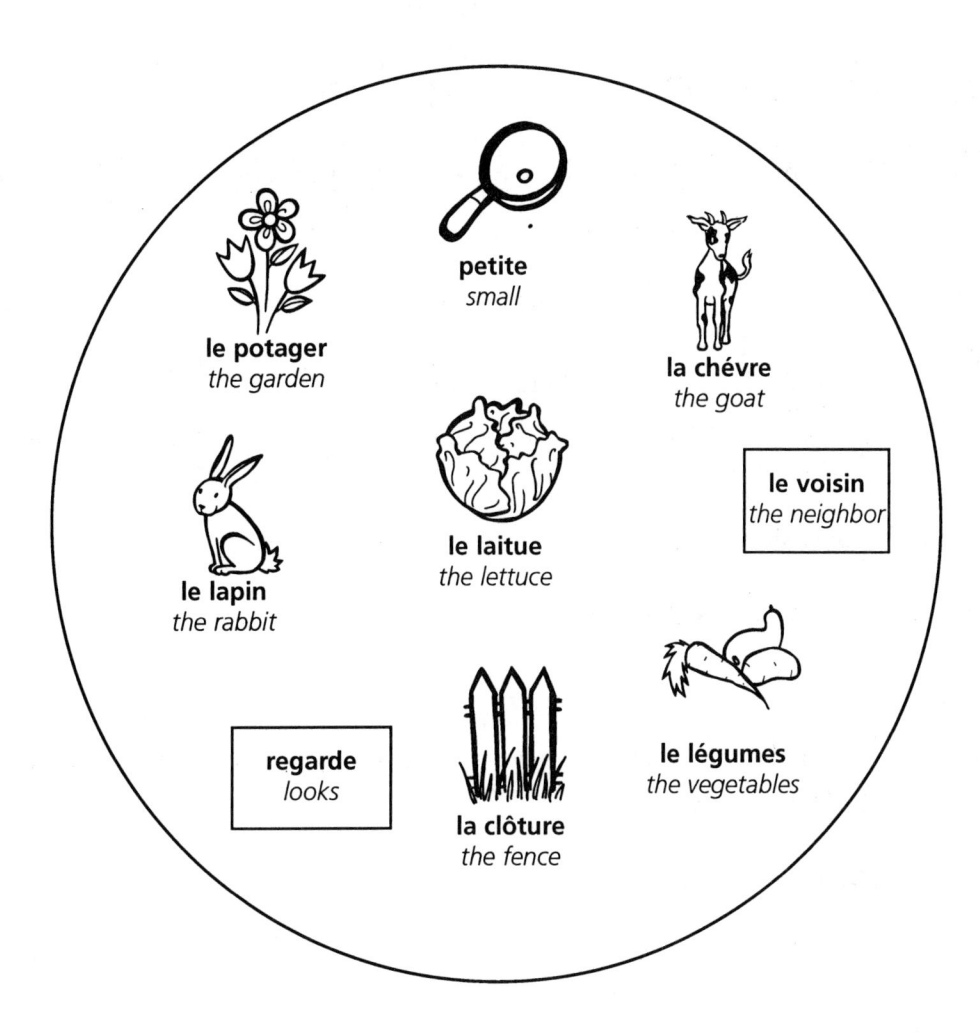

- **le potager** — *the garden*
- **petite** — *small*
- **la chévre** — *the goat*
- **le lapin** — *the rabbit*
- **le laitue** — *the lettuce*
- **le voisin** — *the neighbor*
- **regarde** — *looks*
- **la clôture** — *the fence*
- **le légumes** — *the vegetables*

Word Puzzle 4
(A Boy and His Goat)

Turn the audio on.

Narrator: In the morning, you have quickly packed up all of your things and are ready to go out to the car before you remember you still don't know where you're going.

Tony: Hurry, Grandpa, we need to figure out that puzzle.

Grandpa: Yes, of course. I hope you remember everything from the story, because it looks like those are the words he used here. Let's see if we can figure this out.

Turn the audio off.

Fill in the blanks in the puzzle below by following the numbered clues. The letters that fall in the circled blanks will make additional words that will help you on your adventure.

1. Pride
2. [goat image]
3. [flower image]
4. [fox image]
5. Teeth

1. Rope
2. Plant
3. Fresh

1. [chicken image]
2. [boy image]
3. Dance
4. Who
5. Fence
6. [lettuce image]
7. Neighbor

1. F____
2. chevre
3. potager
4. renard
5. dents

1. Corde
2. _E___
3. plant

1. LEGUMES
2. GARCON
3. DANSE
4. QUI
5. CLOTURE
6. LAITUE
7. VOISIN

"Nous serons dan la galaxie."

Word Puzzle 4 — A Boy and His Goat

A Sandwich in the Universe
(Horseshoe Story)

> 🔊 **Turn the audio on.**

Tony: "Fêtes des Masques." What does that mean?

Grandpa: Of course! "Fêtes des Masques" or, festival of masks, is going on right now in the town of Man, which is north-west of here. That must be where Jean-Paul is heading.

Lisa: Doesn't it seem odd that Malien would take time out from running from the law long enough to go to a party?

Grandpa: You're right. It is a little strange... unless... yes!

Tony: What?

Grandpa: Man must be where he is planning on selling the painting. There will be so many people in town for the festival, that the painting would be almost impossible to trace.

Lisa: If that's true, then we have no time to waste! Hurry, let's go!

Grandpa: Wait... there's something written on the bottom of this puzzle. It says, "Nous serons dans la galaxie."

Tony: What could that mean?

Grandpa: I'm not sure, but I remember the story that goes along with it. Come on, let's get in the car, and I'll tell it to you as we drive.

Narrator: As you leave Yamoussoukro, your Grandpa tells you the story of "Un sandwich dans l'univers."

Un Sandwich dans l'univers...

C'est un sandwich.

C'est l'univers

Dans l'univers, il y a une galaxie.

Dans la galaxie, il y a une étoile.

Près de l'étoile, il y a une planète appelée Terre.

Sur la Terre, il y a un continent.

Sur le continent, il y a un pays.

Dans le pays, il y a une ville.

Dans la ville, il y a un parc.

Dans le parc, Il y a un garçon.

Dans la main du garçon, il y a un sandwich.

Un sandwich dans la main du garçon,

Le garçon dans le parc,

Le parc dans la ville,

La ville dans le pays,

Le pays sur le continent,

Le continent sur la planète appelée Terre,

La Terre près de l'étoile,

L'étoile dans la galaxie,

La galaxie dans l'univers.

Et ici, le sandwich dans la main du garçon.

Turn the audio off.

Performance Challenge:
Create hand actions to represent the actions in the horseshoe story. (For example: Make up different actions to represent the animals you heard about in the story.) After you have created the actions, perform your mini-play for a parent, friend, or one of your bothers and sisters. Remember to narrate your actions in French and then translate your words if your audience does not understand French. For an even greater challenge, try writing your own horseshoe story. Choose several things or people that are related to each other in some way. Think of a chain of events that connects the characters in the story. To finish the story, figure out how the events could be reversed in order to back through the pictures and the plot.

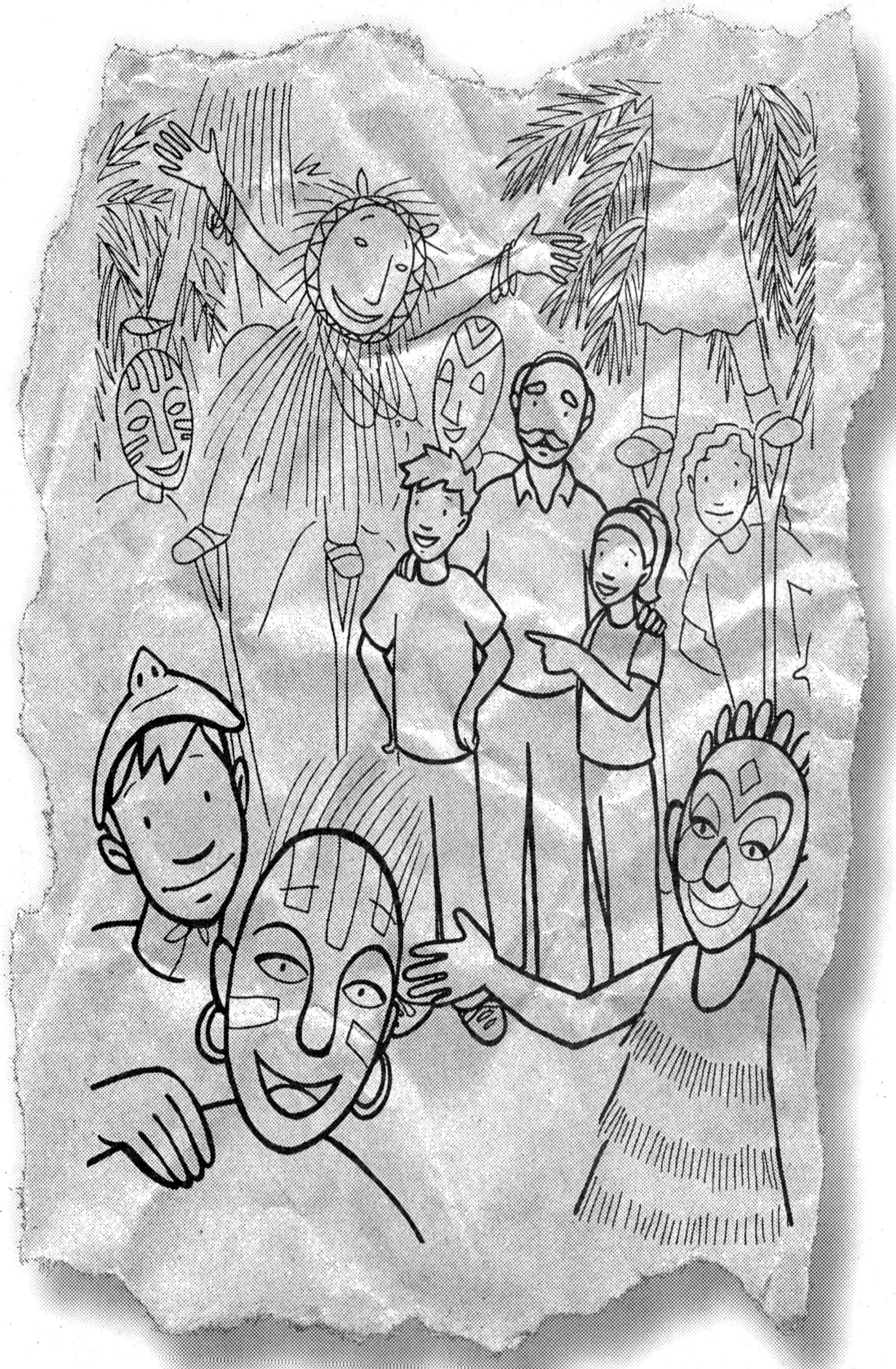

Power-Glide **Children's French Level III**

A Sandwich in the Universe
(Scatter Chart)

🔊 **Turn the audio on.**

Track 24

Narrator: It is late in the morning when you arrive at Man, but the festival is already going on. You see people in masks, both of silk and feathers and of wood, which is a little bit scary. You are fascinated, however, by the Yacouba stilt dancers, who do amazing tricks way up on wooden stilts.

Grandpa: Well, usually I would say that it would be easy to find Jean-Paul here, because it's not a very large town, but with the festival going on, it might be a lot harder.

Lisa: Well, at least we have the clue, even if we don't know what it means.

Tony: Yeah, and we're learning the story, too.

Grandpa: Did you feel like you understood the story?

Lisa: Pretty much, but there were some words I didn't recognize.

Grandpa: Okay, listen carefully.

Look at the pictures on your workbook page and point to what you hear.

Track 25

le sandwich
the sandwich

la galaxie
the galaxy

le parc
the park

la Terre
the earth

la ville
the city

le garçon
the boy

le continent
the continent

la main
the hand

le pays
the country

l'étoile
the star

🔊 **Turn the audio off.**

Performance Challenge:
Choose five of the new words and pictures that you learned in the Scatter Chart. Show the pictures to a parent, friend, or one of your brothers and sisters and explain to them how you think the picture represents the words you have learned. For an even greater challenge, create your own story using the pictures. Bring out the artist in yourself by drawing your own versions of the pictographs and making a book with the story you create.

A Sandwich in the Universe — Scatter Chart

A Sandwich in the Universe
(Horseshoe Story)

Turn the audio on.

Grandpa: Do you feel like you understand the story better now, that you've been through the words?

Tony: Yeah, I think so.

Grandpa: Good.

Narrator: Afternoon is wearing on, and you are beginning to be a little tired and frustrated. Even though the masks aren't too frightening by day, you don't think you want to be out in the festival at night.

Lisa: How are we ever going to find Malien and Jean-Paul, Grandpa?

Grandpa: It's simply a matter of deciphering the clue. For right now, let's focus on the story. To make sure you understood it, I want you to repeat it back to me, using as much French as possible. Okay?

Un Sandwich dans l'univers...

C'est un sandwich.

C'est l'univers

Dans l'univers, il y a une galaxie.

Dans la galaxie, il y a une étoile.

Près de l'étoile, il y a une planète appelée Terre.

Sur la Terre, il y a un continent.

Sur le continent, il y a un pays.

Dans le pays, il y a une ville.

Dans la ville, il y a un parc.

Dans le parc, Il y a un garçon.

Dans la main du garçon, il y a un sandwich.

Un sandwich dans la main du garçon,

Le garçon dans le parc,

Le parc dans la ville,

La ville dans le pays,

Le pays sur le continent,

Le continent sur la planète appelée Terre,

La Terre près de l'étoile,

L'étoile dans la galaxie,

La galaxie dans l'univers.

Et ici, le sandwich dans la main du garçon.

🔊 Turn the audio off.

Performance Challenge:

Create hand actions to represent the actions in the horseshoe story. (For example: Make up different actions to represent the animals you heard about in the story.) After you have created the actions, perform your mini-play for a parent, friend, or one of your bothers and sisters. Remember to narrate your actions in French and then translate your words if your audience does not understand French. For an even greater challenge, try writing your own horseshoe story. Choose several things or people that are related to each other in some way. Think of a chain of events that connects the characters in the story. To finish the story, figure out how the events could be reversed in order to back through the pictures and the plot.

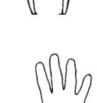

Final Word Puzzle
(A Sandwich in the Universe)

🔊 Turn the audio on.

Grandpa: Good. You've remembered the story very well. All we need to do now is figure out the clue. Do you remember what it was?

Lisa: "Nous serons dans la galaxie."

Grandpa: Right. Now, "in the galaxy" was...

Tony: "Dans la galaxie." The answer must be "galaxie."

Grandpa: Yes, but what could it mean?

Lisa: Look, Grandpa, over there! There's a hotel called "La galaxie." Could that be it?

Grandpa: Of course! Jean-Paul was trying to tell us the hotel where he would be staying.

Narrator: You all quickly run into the hotel, and ask for Jean-Paul's name. The man behind the desk tells you that Jean-Paul and his cousin just checked out, but that Jean-Paul left a message for you. You take the piece of paper, and you see that it is another puzzle.

Grandpa: It looks like it uses the words from "Un sandwich dans la galaxie." Let's see if we can figure it out.

🔊 Turn the audio off.

Power-Glide **Children's French Level III**

Fill in the blanks in the puzzle below by following the numbered clues. The letters that fall in the circled blanks will make additional words that will help you on your adventure.

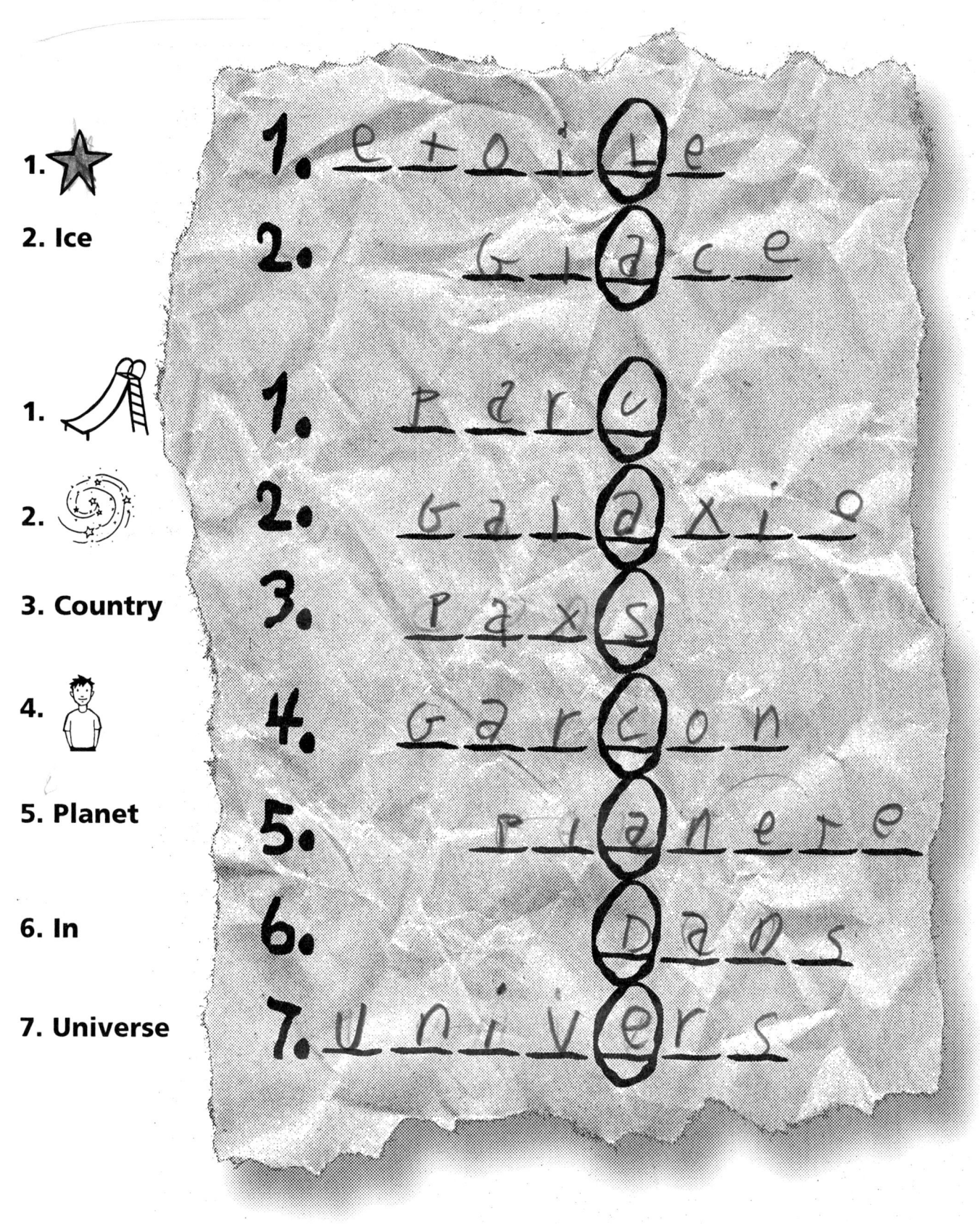

1. ★ — 1. e t o i l **e**
2. Ice — 2. g l **a** c e

1. 🛝 — 1. p a r **c**
2. 🌌 — 2. g a l a x i **e**
3. Country — 3. p a **y** s
4. 👦 — 4. g a r **ç** o n
5. Planet — 5. p l **a** n e t e
6. In — 6. **D** a n s
7. Universe — 7. u n i **v** e r s

Final Word Puzzle — 99 — The Sandwich in the Universe

Power-Glide **Children's French Level III**

Safe Return
(Mission Accomplished)

🔊 **Turn the audio on.**

Lisa: Let's see. The answer is, "La Cascade." What is that?

Narrator: Your grandpa asks the man behind the counter, who tells him it is a famous waterfall outside of town, and he gives you directions. It is almost night when you arrive outside the waterfall and begin to walk into the jungle.

Grandpa: I'm worried. I'm afraid this might be the place that Malien is meeting whoever he is selling the painting to, and if so, we don't have a moment to lose.

Narrator: As you continue into the jungle, you see a man walking toward you, on his way out. At first you don't think anything of it, but as he comes closer, you notice that he is very well dressed, for hiking in the jungle, and that he is holding something under his arm, wrapped in canvas.

Tony: Grandpa, do you see that man?

Lisa: What does he have under his arm?

Grandpa: You don't think that... hold on.

Narrator: Your grandpa approaches the man and begins to speak to him. The man is confused at first , then looks more and more shocked as they continue to talk. After several moments, the man takes out the package from under his arm, and removes the canvas. Underneath is the painting you have been searching for!

Tony: That's the painting! How did he get it?

Grandpa: Well, this man, his name is Victor, is originally from France, and is an avid art collector. Malien contacted him, saying that he was a dealer in rare paintings, and wanted to sell him this one. Victor had no idea that the painting was stolen, and is willing to return it to the museum.

Narrator: Needless to say, you are overjoyed. Victor gives information to the Côte d'Ivoire police that help them apprehend Malien, and everyone is treating you like heroes for finding the stolen paintings. Your parents fly down from Marseilles and beam with pride as you recount all of your adventures in finding the painting. Your grandpa encourages you to prove to them how much French you have learned, and you gladly agree to show them how much you have improved.

🔊 **Turn the audio off.**

Power-Glide **Children's** French Level III

Test 2
(Review)

🔊 **Turn the audio on.**

Track 30

A. Frame Identifications

For each question, you will see a box with pictures. You will hear a statement about one of the pictures. There will be a pause of 10 seconds to identify the picture, and then the statement will be repeated.

1. [four-picture frame: globe, dogs, cat, rabbit — handwritten "Le pain" by rabbit]

2. [four-picture frame: bed, chair, fly — handwritten "Le que", wing]

3.
the eagle *legia*	the woman
the thief	the food

4.
the police	the eagle
the thief	the hunter *le susus*

5. [four-picture frame: sandwich — handwritten "le sandwich", box with arrow, ice cream cone, checkered floor]

Test 2 — 101 — Review

Power-Glide Children's French Level III

Comprehension Multiple-Choice

Complete the following conversations by choosing the correct answer from the options listed.

1. "Dominique! Je suis heureux que vous soyez ici. Ils son mes petits enfants."
   - (A) Enchantée.
   - B. C'est bien fait!
   - C. Allons nous en.
   - D. De rien.

2. Who owned le potager?
   - (A) Le garçon
   - B. La chèvre
   - C. Le voisin
   - D. Madame Renarde

3. Qu'est a qui c'est passé en premier?
   - A. Le chat est venu et a attrapé la souris.
   - B. La femme a préparé la nourriture.
   - C. La chasseur est venu et a attaque le serpent.
   - D. Le policier est venu et a arrêté le voleur.

4. Oú est la galaxie?
   - A. Dans le parc.
   - B. Dans la ville.
   - C. Dans le pays.
   - (D) Dans l'univers.

5. Pourquoi pleures-tu?
   - A. Bien fait! Je mange la nourriture.
   - B. Enchanté. Savez-vous oú je peux trouver ala?
   - (C) La chévre a enfoncé la clôture du voisin et mange la laitue.
   - D. Bien, je ne vois aucun probléme.

Now go on to complete the reading/writing portion of this test.

🔊 **Turn the audio off.**

Matching

Choose the statements that match and draw a line to connect the two.

1. lettuce — C. la laitue
2. fence — E. la clôture
3. garden — A. le potager
4. continent — B. le continent
5. eagle — D. l'aigle

True or False

Write T or F for each statement.

__F__ 1. Le voleur arrests le policier et puts him en prison.

__T__ 2. Le chévre dans l'histoire es afraid du frelon.

__T__ 3. Le voisin has des laitues dans son potager.

__F__ 4. Le chasseur eats l'aigle.

__T__ 5. When none of the autres animaux knew what to do, le frelon saved the day.

Test 2   Review

Born 1996

Answer Key

1.

🌍	🐕
🐈	🐇

2.

🛏️	🪑
🪰	🏐

3.

the eagle	the woman
the thief	the food

4.

the police	the eagle
the thief	the hunter

5.

🥪	⬆️
🍦	▨

Comprehension Multiple-Choice
1. A.
2. C.
3. B.
4. D.
5. C.

Matching
1. C
2. E
3. A
4. B
5. D

True or False
1. F
2. T
3. T
4. F
5. T

Recipes

BLANC MANGER

    2 tbsp unflavored gelatin

    1/2 cup cold water

    6 egg yolks

    2/3 cup sugar

    2 cup milk

    2 cups coconut milk

    1/8 tsp salt

    1 tsp vanilla

Soak gelatin in cold water. Beat the egg yolks thoroughly, then add the sugar a little at a time. In a medium saucepan, cook the milk and the coconut milk just until it starts steaming—don't boil! Slowly add the egg mixture to the milk mixture, and stir to combine. Scald the milk and slowly add to the egg and sugar mixture. Then place this mixture in a double boiler over hot water. Cook it, stirring constantly, until it smoothly coats a metal spoon. Remove the mix from the heat. Add the gelatin mix, and stir until it's thoroughly dissolved. Stir in the salt and vanilla, then pour it into a greased mold. Refrigerate it until firm, at least 7 hours or overnight. You can serve it plain, or with berries and cream. Yummy!

KEDJENOU

    3 lbs chicken pieces, skinned

    1 eggplant, chopped into bite-size pieces

    2 large onions, minced

    2 red or green peppers, coarsely diced

    4 tomatoes, coarsely diced

    1 small piece ginger root, finely chopped

    1/2 tsp thyme

    1 bay leaf

    1 tbsp peanut oil (can substitute vegetable or sesame oil)

    salt and pepper to taste

Combine all ingredients in a large pot. Cover the pot tightly so that no moisture can escape. Cook over medium-low heat or on hot coals for 45 minutes. During cooking, it's traditional to shake the pot occasionally so that nothing sticks. (Be careful! It's hot.)